brotherhood
of
darkness

Love Dad
7-19-2011

I dedicate this book to Barbara, who stands beside me in all that I do, and to David, our son, who works with us selflessly. I also want to acknowledge those who support our ministry and strive to promote revival among God's people.

All Scripture quotations are from the King James Version of the Holy Bible.

Printed in the United States of America

ISBN 978-1-57558-063-0

brotherhood of darkness

Dr. Stanley Monteith

Guiding the way through the darkness

RADIO LIBERTY
Host: "Dr. Stan" Monteith

P.O. Box 969, Soquel, CA 95073   800-544-8927

In 1962, Dr. Stanley Monteith began studying the covert organizations that are working to establish world government. When he retired from medicine in 1994, he created Radio Liberty which is heard on radio, Internet, satellite, and shortwave.

Shortwave, satellite, and radio frequencies are listed at www.radioliberty.com.

Internet programs are broadcast on:

> www.radioliberty.com
> www.genlive.com
> www.americanewsnet.com
> www.soundwaves2000.com

Dr. Monteith writes a monthly newsletter that can be read at www.radioliberty.com or purchased by subscription by calling 800-544-8927.

table of contents

Foreword

This book is the result of thirty-eight years of travel, study, and research. It is a story of mass murder, cruelty, and inhumanity, yet it offers hope to those who believe in the promise of salvation. Very few people have heard of some of the esoteric societies and arcane organizations that are discussed, because they have cleverly concealed their existence from public scrutiny.

This story will change the way you look at the world, motivate you to reevaluate what is important, and change your life forever. I hope you will want to help me distribute *Brotherhood of Darkness* and join the spiritual battle that is currently being waged to determine the course of Western civilization.

Chapter One

the dark Porces

An understanding of the forces that have shaped the events of the twentieth century is predicated not on facts to be learned, but rather on secrets to be discovered.

—Author Unknown

The invisible society is a secret and most august fraternity whose members are dedicated to the service of a mysterious arcanum arcanorum.

—Lectures on Ancient Philosophy[1]

The story you are about to read is incredible but true. It will challenge everything you believe. It is about secret societies, how they have directed the course of civilization and how they influence your life today. Most people don't realize they exist because their minds have been conditioned to reject any thought of such organizations. Manly P. Hall was often cited as "one of the foremost authorities on esoteric philosophy," and when he died *The Scottish Rite Journal* referred to him as "Masonry's Greatest Philosopher."[2] In his book, *The Secret Teachings of All Ages*, he traced the history of esoteric societies through the ages and revealed that they have left hidden clues to their existence in pictures, woodcuts, books, and architecture. You see their symbols every day, but don't recognize them. Whenever you look at the back of a dollar bill you see their emblem, but you don't realize that it represents the Mystery Religions of antiquity.[3]

I want to introduce you to three concepts and three poems that will help you understand the story you are about to read.

The first concept is:

An understanding of the forces that have shaped the events of the twentieth century is predicated not on facts to be learned, but rather on secrets to be discovered.

—Author unknown

I have studied history for over fifty years, and the longer I live the more convinced I have become that it is impossible to grasp what is taking place today without an understanding of the secret societies. As you read this book, you will learn about a number of them, and how they have fashioned the modern world.

The second concept is:

Men and women become accomplices to those evils they fail to oppose.

—Author unknown

Once you recognize what is happening, you have a moral obligation to become involved. Perhaps all you can do is tell others, write letters, or contribute financially to those who are working to expose what is taking place. If you choose to do nothing, you become an accomplice to evil, and one day you will have to answer for your failure to act.

The third concept is:

The price that good people pay for their apathy and indifference to public affairs is that they are ruled by evil men.
—Author unknown

Only half of evangelical Christians are registered to vote, and only half of those registered actually do vote. We must convince everyone they have a moral obligation to become involved in the political process, ensure honest elections, and insist that elected representatives obey the Constitution. Unless enough people are willing to take action, we will surely lose our freedom.

Each of the following poems reflects an aspect of the spiritual struggle that is taking place.

The first poem was written in 1842 by Alfred Lord Tennyson. It is often quoted by those who advocate world federation.

The second poem was written in 1902 by Rudyard Kipling to honor the man who is responsible for many of our current problems.

The third poem was written before the Civil War by James Russell Lowell.

I will address each poem in turn.

When I mention Alfred Lord Tennyson, most people remember his poem, "The Charge of the Light Brigade."

Half a league, half a league,
Half a league onward,
All in the valley of Death

Rode the six hundred.
"Forward, the Light Brigade!
Charge for the guns!" he said:
Into the valley of Death
    Rode the six hundred.

"Forward, the light Brigade!"
Was there a man dismayed?
Not tho' the soldiers knew
    Someone had blundered:
Theirs not to make reply,
Theirs not to reason why,
Theirs but to do and die:
Into the valley of Death
    Rode the six hundred.

Cannon to the right of them,
Cannon to the left of them,
Cannon in front of them
    Volley'd and thunder'd;
Storm'd at with shot and shell,
Boldly they rode and well,
Into the jaws of Death,
Into the mouth of hell
    Rode the six hundred.

Flash'd all their sabres bare,
Flash'd as they turned in air
Sab'ring the gunners there,
Charging an army, while
    All the world wondered.
Plunged in the battery-smoke,
Right through the line they broke;
Cossack and Russian

Reel'd from the sabre-stroke
  Shattered and sundered.
Then they rode back, but not—
  Not the six hundred.

Cannon to the right of them,
Cannon to the left of them,
Cannon behind them
  Volleyed and thundered;
Stormed at with shot and shell,
While horse and hero fell,
They that had fought so well
Came thro' the jaws of Death,
Back from the mouth of Hell,
All that was left of them,
  Left of six hundred.

When can their glory fade?
Oh, the wild charge they made!
  All the world wondered.
Honor the charge they made!
Honor the Light Brigade,
  Noble Six Hundred!

These were memorable verses, but most people have never heard of Lord Tennyson's most important poem, "Locksley Hall." He wrote it to popularize his belief that Great Britain had a moral obligation to consolidate the world under British rule. I suspect that he had no idea his poem would have a lasting impact, or that it would be responsible for many of the tragic events of the twentieth century. I also suspect that he had no concept of the true nature of the dark spiritual forces he had engaged, or how those forces influenced his view of the world.[4]

The poem "Locksley Hall" is discussed in volume 17 of the 1966 edition of the *Encyclopedia Americana*. The remainder of Lord Tennyson's poetry, and his biography, are covered in volume 26. Why is that important? Because those who work within the shadows understand the significance of the message contained in "Locksley Hall," and felt it should be covered separately. The author who wrote the analysis of "Locksley Hall" in volume 17 noted that it prophesied "universal peace by means of a league of nations." That has been the goal of the arcane societies since the dawn of civilization, and it remains their objective today.[5]

I will quote only the most important sections of "Locksley Hall":

> For I dipt into the future,
>   far as human eye could see,
> Saw the Vision of the world,
>   and all the wonder that would be;
> Heard the heavens fill with shouting,
>   and there rain'd a ghastly dew
> From the nations' airy navies
>   grappling in the central blue;
>
> Till the war-drum throbb'd no longer,
>   and the battle-flags were furl'd
> In the Parliament of man,
>   the Federation of the world.
> There the common sense of most
>   shall hold a fretful realm in awe,
> And the kindly earth shall slumber,
>   lapt in universal law.[6]

Thirty years after Lord Tennyson penned those words, Professor John Ruskin, who taught at Oxford University, embraced Tennyson's vision. John Ruskin was a charismatic teacher who had the ability to project his concepts into the minds of his students. He used his lectures to convince his students that they had a moral obligation to disseminate English culture and unite the world under British rule.[7] Many of the young men who sat in his classes were enthralled by his ideas, and they dedicated their lives to fulfilling his dream. When they graduated, many of them entered government service, and by the early 1900s they held strategic positions in the English government. They were the men who were responsible for creating, and then prolonging, World War I. Why would rational men want a long and bloody conflict? Because they realized that countries would never relinquish their national sovereignty unless they recognized the futility of war, and World War I convinced most people that war was futile. Over twenty million people perished in that senseless carnage. Repeated efforts to end the conflict were blocked, and when the war finally ended, most people and most nations were ready to cede their sovereignty to the League of Nations. I will develop that concept further in chapter four when I discuss Winston Churchill and the part he played in determining military strategy in both World War I and World War II.[8]

Other people embraced Lord Tennyson's vision. Edward Bellamy wrote *Looking Backward: 2000–1887* in 1888, and he advocated socialism and world government. His story began in Boston in 1887 when a young man fell asleep after taking a sleeping potion and awoke in the year 2000 to find the world transformed into a socialist Utopia. Bellamy described the world he envisioned with the advent of the new millennium, and his predictions were truly remarkable when you consider that he lived over a hundred years ago. He wrote:

> An American credit card . . . is just as good in Europe as
> American gold used to be, and on precisely the same con-
> dition, namely, that it be exchanged into the currency of
> the country you are traveling in. An American in Berlin
> takes his credit card to the local office of the international
> council . . . the amount being charged against the United
> States in favor of Germany on the international account.[9]

How could Edward Bellamy have foreseen what is taking
place today? Was he privy to some source of secret knowledge? He foresaw large corporations taken over by larger
corporations until finally all commerce was merged into a
single corporation, The Great Trust.

> The nation . . . organized as the one great business corpo-
> ration in which all other corporations were absorbed; it
> became the one capitalist in the place of all other capital-
> ists, the sole employer, the final monopoly in which all
> previous and lesser monopolies were swallowed up, a mo-
> nopoly in the profits and economies of which all citizens
> shared. The epoch of trusts had ended in The Great Trust.[10]

Edward Bellamy foresaw what is taking place in communist
China where all Chinese corporations are answerable to the
state. He described the social welfare programs that exist in
the United States today, and he envisioned the coming world
government when he wrote:

> . . . I, who, having beheld in a vision the world I looked on,
> sang of it in words that again and again, during these last
> wondrous days, had rung in my mind: —
> For I dipt into the future, far as human eye could see,
> .Saw the vision of the world, and all the wonder that
> would be;

> Till the war-drum throbb'd no longer, And the battle
>   flags were furled.
> In the Parliament of man, the federation of the world.
> Then the common sense of most shall hold a fretful
>   realm in awe,
> And the kindly earth shall slumber, lapt in universal
>   law.[11]

Shortly after his book was published, Bellamy Clubs began forming across the United States. As the movement for socialism and world government spread, a number of wealthy men embraced Bellamy's concepts. Among them was Andrew Carnegie. Most people think of him as a "robber baron," an example of everything wrong with the free enterprise system. That view is incorrect. Andrew Carnegie didn't believe in free enterprise. He believed in monopoly capitalism which allows those of great wealth to use government to exploit others. Andrew Carnegie was a socialist, but the socialism he envisioned created a ruling class. After selling U.S. Steel, he funded several foundations with instructions that their grant-making power was to be used to transform society and promote world government. Why did Andrew Carnegie support those goals? Because he recognized that socialism is a sincere, benevolent, idealistic theory, but it doesn't work without force. Under socialism the government takes from each according to their ability and gives to others according to their need. Everyone is controlled by the government; the government is controlled by politicians, and politicians are bought and sold by wealthy men and corporations. That is why Andrew Carnegie, and other men of great wealth, favor socialism.[12]

Andrew Carnegie embraced Lord Tennyson's vision in 1893 in his book *Triumphant Democracy,* when he wrote:

The Parliament of Man and the Federation of the World have already been hailed by the poet, and these mean a step much farther in advance of the proposed reunion of Britain and America. . . . I say that as surely as the sun in the heavens once shown upon Britain and America unit-ed, so surely is it one morning to rise, shine upon, and greet again the reunited state, "The British–American Union." [13]

One hundred years later, Arthur Schlesinger, Jr. wrote an article that appeared on the editorial page of the *Wall Street Journal*. In October 1993 many people were concerned because we seemed to be relinquishing our national sovereignty, and moving toward world government and a New World Order. Arthur Schlesinger, Jr. addressed that concern:

The world of law will not be attained by exhortation. . . . Let us not kid ourselves that we can have a new world order without paying for it in blood as well as in money. Maybe the costs of enforcement are too great. National interest narrowly construed may well be the safer rule. But let us recognize that we are surrendering a noble dream. Remember those lines of Tennyson that Churchill called "the most wonderful of modern prophesies" and that Harry Truman carried in his wallet throughout his life:

For I dipt into the future, far as human eye could see, Saw the Vision of the world, and all the wonder that would be. Heard the heavens fill with shouting, and there rain'd a ghastly dew From the nations' airy navies grappling in the central blue . . .

**Till the war-drum throbb'd no longer, and the battle flags
were furl'd**
In the Parliament of Man, the Federation of the World.[14]

Here Arthur Schlesinger, Jr. revealed the little-known fact
that both Winston Churchill and Harry Truman were dedicated to world government. Did Winston Churchill really want
Great Britain to surrender its national sovereignty? Why did
Harry Truman carry Lord Tennyson's poem in his wallet
throughout his life? Is it possible that both men were members of the arcane societies?

Most people have forgotten the strange things that happened during Harry Truman's presidency. First, he signed the
United Nations Charter, knowing full well that the U.N. was
designed to become the government of the world. Then he
ceded control of Eastern Europe and China to the communists, and when the public began to question why he had betrayed hundreds of millions of people to a life of slavery, he
plunged us into a no-win war in Asia. When General Mac-
Arthur told a congressman that he wasn't allowed to win the
Korean War, President Truman relieved him of his command.[15]
If you study that era, you will discover that General Lin Piao,
the communist leader who commanded the Chinese army
that attacked our soldiers in North Korea, knew there was a
secret agreement that precluded us from winning the Korean War. General Lin Piao wrote:

**I would never have made the attack and risked my men
and military reputation if I had not been assured that Washington would restrain General MacArthur from taking
adequate retaliatory measures against my lines of supply
and communication.**[16]

At this point, I want to explain how Harry Truman brought communism to China. Most people believe that the Nationalist Chinese lost the civil war, but nothing could be further from the truth. General Chiang Kai-shek's armies were winning the civil war until the American State Department placed an arms embargo on the Nationalist forces which prevented them from buying weapons or supplies anywhere in the world. Even the weapons they had previously purchased on Okinawa and other Pacific islands were blockaded. How can an army fight without weapons? It can't. Contrary to everything you have heard or read, our State Department intentionally brought Chairman Mao to power. To verify that charge, I quote from a long-suppressed Senate report on the fall of China. Copies of the pages quoted are available to researchers:

INSTITUTE OF PACIFIC RELATIONS REPORT

of the

Committee on the Judiciary

Eighty-Second Congress

Second Session

S.(enate) Res.(olution) 366

A Resolution Relating to the Internal

Security of the United States

At the end of 1945 when General Marshall left for China, the balance of power was with the Chinese Nationalists . . . and remained so until at least June 1946. . . . Chiang's divisions were chasing the Communists northward and the prospect of victory by Nationalist China was at its highest. . . . However, when General Marshall arrived in China, he undertook to bring about the coalition government which his directive demanded. . . . This plan failed when coalition failed. . . .

When the Chinese government did not effect coalition, by the summer of 1946 United States military assistance to China was brought to an end. Not only did the United States stop sending military supplies to the Chinese Government; the shipment of war materials actually purchased by the Chinese also was halted. . . . The Chinese also had purchased surplus equipment that remained on Okinawa and other Pacific islands. Even the shipment of this was banned. . . . A complete embargo took effect in the summer of 1946. It was maintained at least until May 1947. General Chennault testified that the first shipment arrived in Shanghai in December 1948. . . . Chennault further stated that the war material sent to China after the embargo did not arrive in time to aid the Chinese Nationalists in the field. . . . Admiral Cooke . . . testified that the Chinese had a number of divisions equipped with American arms. . . . When the flow of American ammunition was stopped, these divisions lost their fire power and were defeated. Even after the Eightieth Congress appropriated $125,000,000 for aid to the Chinese, shipments were delayed and when the guns finally reached the Chinese general in north China they were without bolts and therefore useless.[17]

Why did our State Department send the Nationalist Chinese guns without bolts? Could that have happened by accident? It is impossible to read the complete text of the McCarran Committee Report without coming to the conclusion that the Truman Administration betrayed the Nationalist Chinese and brought Chairman Mao to power. Why? Could it have had anything to do with the fact that Harry Truman carried Lord Tennyson's poem in his wallet throughout his life?

I encountered the second poem when I visited my son in Cape Town in the mid-1970s. As we drove down the coastal highway that winds along the base of Table Mountain, I saw a small, gray replica of the Lincoln Memorial nestled against the hillside. I was curious, so we trudged up the dusty path that led to the front of the granite monument. Stone lions guarded both sides of the stairway before us. After climbing the stairs, we passed between granite pillars and entered an area that contained a stone pedestal. On the top of the pedestal sat a larger-than-life bust of a man. The expression on the stone face was stern, the eyes hollowed so their gaze followed us wherever we moved. As the cold Atlantic wind blew past the pillars behind us, I saw a poem engraved on the pedestal:

The intense and brooding spirit still,
Shall quicken and control.
Living he was the land,
And dead, his soul shall be her soul.

Rudyard Kipling penned those words in 1902, and they were read at Cecil John Rhodes' funeral. To quicken is to come back to life after dying, and if there was ever a man whose legacy lived on after his death, it was Cecil John Rhodes. What most people don't realize is that his legacy continues to dominate Europe and Africa, and his influence casts a dark shadow over our nation today.

The names of most of the men who have tried to unite the world are well known: Nimrod, Nebuchadnezzar, Genghis Khan, Alexander the Great, Julius Caesar, Napoleon, Hitler, Lenin, Stalin, and Chairman Mao. On the other hand, very few people associate the name of Rhodes with the current effort to establish a world government. It is well known, however, to his followers and members of the arcane societies. In 1877, Cecil John Rhodes laid out his plan to unite the world under Anglo-Saxon rule. He knew he would never live to see his undertaking completed, but he dedicated his life to that cause, and he recruited others to carry on his program after his death.[18] Cecil John Rhodes has done more to unite the world than any other man in history. When he was a student at Oxford University, he attended John Ruskin's inaugural lecture, and he was so impressed with Ruskin's concepts that he wrote them down in longhand and carried them with him the rest of his life, just as Harry Truman carried Lord Tennyson's poem in his wallet throughout his life.[19]

Cecil Rhodes wrote a *Confession of Faith* in 1877. There he laid out his plan to bring the world under British rule and recapture the United States. He wrote:

> **The idea gleaming and dancing before ones eyes like a will-o-the-wisp at last frames itself into a plan. Why should we not form a secret society with but one object, the furtherance of the British Empire, for the bringing of the whole uncivilized world under British rule, for the recovery of the United States, for the making [of] the Anglo-Saxon race but one Empire. . . .[20]**

Cecil Rhodes acquired the major gold and diamond mines of southern Africa and used his wealth to pursue his dream. In 1891, he established a secret society. When he realized that he wouldn't live to see his vision fulfilled, he left his vast fortune to the Rhodes Trust to fund his secret society and the Rhodes Scholarship Fund.[21]

During the past century over forty-six hundred young men have been sent to Oxford University where they were indoctrinated in socialism and world government. President Bill Clinton, General Wesley Clark, Strobe Talbot, Senator Bill Bradley, and thousands of other prominent men are Rhodes Scholars. They work in government offices, in international

banks, on the boards of corporations, in tax-exempt foundations, in the Supreme Court, in the media, in our universities, in the United Nations Association, and in the Council on
Foreign Relations. At Oxford they became part of an elite
group that was dedicated to changing the world. That is why
Cecil Rhodes' spirit still quickens and controls, and why his
influence still casts a dark shadow over our nation.[22]

The third poem was written by James Russell Lowell to
address the problem of slavery. The version cited is taken from
the hymn, "Once to Every Man and Nation":

> **Once to every man and nation**
>   **Comes the moment to decide,**
> **In the strife of truth with falsehood,**
>   **for the good or evil side. . . .**
> **Then it is the brave man chooses,**
>   **While the coward stands aside,**
> **'Til the multitude make virtue**
>   **Of the faith they had denied. . . .**
> **Though the cause of evil prosper,**
>   **Yet 'tis truth alone is strong;**
> **Though her portion be the scaffold**
>   **And upon the throne be wrong,**
> **Yet that scaffold sways the future,**
>   **And, behind the dim unknown,**
> **Standeth God within the shadow,**
>   **Keeping watch above his own . . .**[23]

Here James Russell Lowell described the struggle that began
in the Garden of Eden and continues to this day. It is a battle
between truth and falsehood, between good and evil, between
Light and Darkness, between God and Satan. It has been going
on for six thousand years, and it will continue until the end

of time.

The past two centuries have been the most violent period in recorded history. Who is responsible for the terrible wars and bloody revolutions that have plagued the world? Why did the United States Supreme Court take God and prayer out of our schools? Why can't we do something about the moral depravity that is destroying our nation?

When you complete this book you will know the answer to those questions, and you will never look at the world in the same way again.

Footnotes

1. Manly P. Hall, *Lectures On Ancient Philosophy*, Philosophical Research Society, Inc. Los Angeles, California, p. 433.
2. Ralph Epperson, *Masonry: Conspiracy Against Christianity*, Publius Press, 1997, p. 18.
3. Manly P. Hall, *The Secret Teachings of All Ages*, Philosophical Research Society, California, pp. III–V.
4. Dennis Cuddy, *Now Is the Dawning of the New Age New World Order*, Hearthstone Publishing Ltd., Oklahoma City, Oklahoma, 1991, p. 38. Dr. Cuddy told me that Lord Tennyson belonged to the Society for Psychical Research which was organized by Tennyson's uncle.
5. *Encyclopedia Americana*, International Edition, Americana Corporation, New York, Volume 17, p. 643.
6. Charles Johnson, *One Hundred & One Famous Hymns*, Hallberg Publishing Corporation, Delavan, Wisconsin, 1982, p. 87.
7. Carroll Quigley, *Tragedy and Hope: A History of the World in Our Time*, The Macmillan Company, New York, 1966, pp. 130–138.
8. John McManus, *Changing Commands*, The John Birch Society, Appleton, Wisconsin, p. 87. See also "The Nor-

man Dodd Interview," Radio Liberty, P.O. Box 13, Santa Cruz, California, 95063.

9. Edward Bellamy, *Looking Backward*, Dover Publications, Inc., New York, originally published in 1888, republished by Dover in 1996, p. 70.

10. Ibid., p. 27.

11. Ibid., p. 73.

12. Andrew Carnegie, *Triumphant Democracy*, Charles Scribner's Sons, New York, 1893, pp. 530–49.

13. Ibid.

14. Arthur Schlesinger, Jr, "Bye, Bye, Woodrow," *Wall Street Journal*, October 23, 1993, editorial page.

15. For those who would like to understand the Korean War era, I suggest General MacArthur's *Reminiscences*, General Mark Clark's *From the Danube to the Yalu*, Major General Courtney Whitney's *MacArthur: His Rendezvous with History*, and Major Arch Roberts's *Victory Denied*.

16. General Douglas MacArthur, *Reminiscences*, McGraw-Hill Book Company, New York, 1964, p. 375.

17. Institute of Pacific Relations: Report of the Committee of the Judiciary, 82nd Congress, S. Res. 366, pp. 204-205.

18. Frank Aydelotte, *The Vision of Cecil Rhodes*, Oxford University Press, 1946, Preface, p. v.

19. Carroll Quigley, op cit., p. 130.

20. Cecil Rhodes, *Rhodes Confession of Faith*, found among Lord Milner's papers, or available in *The Sustainable Development Syllabus*, P. O. Box 13, Santa Cruz, California 95063.

21. Carroll Quigley, op cit., p. 130.

22. Rhodes Trust, Register of Rhodes Scholars 1903–1995, 1996, ISBN 0-9527695-0-6. Lists 4,600 Rhodes Scholars. See also: Frank Aydelotte, op cit., p. 129.

23. Charles Johnson, op cit.

Chapter Two

too many clues

The plot of Agatha Christie's novel, *Murder on the Orient Express*, will help you understand the story of The Brotherhood of Darkness. The murder took place on the elegant passenger train that traveled between Istanbul and Paris, linking the mystery of the East with the rationalism of the West. Agatha Christie's book was eventually made into a motion picture with Lauren Bacall, Ingrid Bergman, Jacqueline Bisset, Martin Balsam, Sean Connery, Anthony Perkins, Vanessa Redgrave, Richard Widmark, and Albert Finney who played the part of Inspector Poirot. Shortly after the movie began, a group of passengers boarded the Orient Express in Istanbul. Among them was Inspector Hercule Poirot, a world-famous

Belgian detective, and Mr. Ratchet, a wealthy man traveling with his secretary and butler. Shortly after the train departed, Mr. Ratchet approached Inspector Poirot and told him that someone had threatened to kill him. He offered the Inspector fifteen thousand dollars to protect him until they reached Paris, but Inspector Poirot refused. The train entered a tunnel, the movie screen went black, and when the lights came back on, Mr. Ratchet had disappeared. The next morning he was found stabbed to death in his compartment. A railroad official asked Inspector Poirot to solve the crime, so he went to Mr. Ratchet's compartment and began searching for clues. Everywhere he looked he found conflicting evidence, and he suddenly realized that the murder scene had been staged to confuse him. At that point he paused, surveyed the crime scene, and commented:

"There are too many clues."

In many respects that is what is happening today. We are threatened by terrorism, biological warfare, environmental catastrophe, global warming, acid rain, water shortages, nuclear attack, aliens from outer space, genetically altered foods, Y2K, new diseases, an imploding social system, rising crime, moral decay, a failing educational system, and dozens of other real or imagined dangers. When we try to determine who, or what, is responsible for our problems, we are overwhelmed with facts and become confused. Psychologists call our condition cognitive dissonance. Pavlov produced a similar state in dogs. He found that if he conditioned them to salivate in response to the sound of a buzzer, then conditioned them to salivate in response to the sound of a bell, and then conditioned them to salivate in response to a third sound, when all three sounds were transmitted together, the animals became confused and withdrew from reality.[2]

Pavlov's dogs lived in a laboratory where they were monitored. We live in a society where almost everything we see, hear, and read is monitored by those who control the media. Before we can confront our problems effectively, we must understand that someone, or some group, is manipulating our reality. We must free ourselves from their control and discover the truth.

Who Is Responsible for What Is Happening in the World Today?

The Bankers

I am afraid the ordinary citizen will not like to be told that the banks can, and do, create money. . . . And they who control the credit of the nation direct the policy of Governments and hold in the hollow of their hands the destiny of the people.[3]

Many people believe that the bankers are responsible for our problems because they have the ability to create money and either lend it at exorbitant rates or use it to purchase industries, media outlets, property, or politicians. President Thomas Jefferson warned us about the danger of modern banking practices almost two hundred years ago when he wrote:

Everything predicted by the enemies of banks, in the beginning, is now coming to pass. We are to be ruined now by a deluge of bank paper, as we were formerly by the old Continental paper. It is cruel that such revolutions in private fortunes should be at the mercy of avaricious adventurers, who instead of employing their capital, if any they have, in manufactures, commerce, and other useful pur-

suits, make it an instrument to burden all the interchang-
es of property with their swindling profits, profits which
are the price of no useful industry of theirs. Prudent men
must be on their guard in this game of Robin's alive, and
take care that the spark does not extinguish in their hands.
I am an enemy to all banks discounting bills or notes for
anything but coin. But our whole country is so fascinated
by this Jack o' lantern wealth, that they will not stop short
of its total and fatal explosion.[4]

When President Clinton accepted the presidential nomination for the Democratic Party on July 16, 1992, he said:

As a teenager I heard John Kennedy's summons to citizen-
ship. And then, as a student at Georgetown, I heard that
call clarified by a professor named Carroll Quigley. . . .[5]

Who was Carroll Quigley, and why is he important? He was a
liberal university professor who taught at both Princeton and
Harvard before taking a permanent position at Georgetown
University. Unlike other historians who simply record past
events, he wanted to know why things happened. In an effort
to understand the tragic events of the twentieth century, he
spent twenty years researching the men who ruled England
and the United States between 1870 and 1960. He wrote about
them in *Tragedy and Hope: A History of the World in Our Time.*
The Macmillan Company published his book, but shortly after it was released another publisher bought Macmillan and
promptly destroyed the plates to the first half of Professor
Quigley's book. Thousands of people had ordered copies, but
the new publisher refused to reprint it. If you find that diffi-
cult to believe, I offer skeptics a copy of an interview with
Professor Quigley in which he discusses the suppression of

his book.[6] I am personally indebted to him for his research, because without the information he amassed I would never have discovered the Brotherhood of Darkness.

Why is banking important? Professor Quigley explained:

This power of the Bank of England and of its governor was admitted by most qualified observers. In January, 1924, Reginald McKenna, who had been chancellor of the Exchequer in 1915–1916, as chairman of the board of the Midland Bank, told its stockholders: "I am afraid the ordinary citizen will not like to be told that the banks can, and do, create money. . . . And they who control the credit of the nation direct the policy of Governments and hold in the hollow of their hands the destiny of the people." [7]

When I was involved in a research project at Yale University, I came across a letter that President Roosevelt sent to Colonel Edward Mandell House on November 21, 1933. In those days, J. P. Morgan was one of the most powerful financiers in the world. President Roosevelt wrote:

I had a nice talk with Jack Morgan the other day. . . . The real truth of the matter is, as you and I know, that a financial element in the larger centers has owned the Government ever since the days of Andrew Jackson—and I am not wholly excepting the Administration of W. W. [8]

The reference to W. W. referred to President Woodrow Wilson.

Shortly after World War I began, our newspapers started printing stories about German atrocities. They claimed that German soldiers were cutting off the hands of Belgian boys, raping Belgian women and cutting off their breasts. The stories continued until people believed them and felt we had a moral obligation to intervene in the war. Why did newspapers print those stories?

On February 9, 1917, Congressman Oscar Callaway inserted the following statement in the *Congressional Record*.

In March, 1915, the J. P. Morgan interests . . . and their subsidiary organizations, got together 12 men high up in the newspaper world and employed them to select the most influential newspapers in the United States and sufficient number of them to control generally the policy of the daily press of the United States. These 12 men worked the problem out by selecting 179 newspapers, and then began, by an elimination process, to retain only those necessary for the purpose of controlling the general policy of the daily press throughout the country. They found it was only necessary to purchase the control of 25 of the greatest papers. The 25 papers were agreed upon; emissaries were sent to purchase the policy, national and international, of these papers; an agreement was reached; the policy of the papers was bought, to be paid for by the month; an editor was furnished for each paper to properly supervise and edit information regarding the questions of preparedness, militarism, financial policies, and other things of national and international nature considered vital to the interests of the purchasers. This contract is in existence at the present time, and it accounts for the news columns of the daily press of the country being filled with all sorts of preparedness arguments. . . .[9]

By 1917, J. P. Morgan and his associates controlled twenty-five of our most influential newspapers. The atrocity stories were designed to raise public support for American entry into World War I.

Many years later, I met a man who joined the army and went to Europe because he believed he had a moral obligation to try to stop the German atrocities. When the war ended, most of his friends were either dead or injured, but he still believed the war was justified until he learned there were no mutilated Belgian boys or raped Belgian women. With tears in his eyes, he told me how devastated he was when he realized that everything he believed had been a lie.

J. P. Morgan and his associates manipulated the United States into World War I. Are the bankers responsible for what is happening today?

The Central Bankers

> . . . the powers of financial capitalism had another far-reaching aim, nothing less than to create a world system of financial control in private hands able to dominate the political system of each country and the economy of the world as a whole.
>
> —Professor Carroll Quigley[10]

Although there is a great deal of evidence to support the theory that bankers are responsible for what is happening, some people contend that the central banks are the real problem. They note that every nation has a privately owned central bank, and that every central bank in the world is affiliated with the Bank for International Settlements.

Dr. Dennis Cuddy wrote about that organization in his book, *Secret Records Revealed:*

> On August 5, 1995, the *New York Times* published an article by Keith Bradsher, in which he wrote:
> "In a small Swiss city sits an international organization so obscure and secretive. . . . Control of the institu-

tion, the Bank for International Settlements, lies with some of the world's most powerful and least visible men: the heads of thirty-two central banks, officials able to shift billions of dollars and alter the course of economies at the stroke of a pen."[11]

On June 28, 1998, the *Washington Post* published an article about the Bank for International Settlements (BIS) titled, "At Secret Meetings in Switzerland, 13 People Shape the World's Economy," which described these individuals as "this economic cabal . . . this secretive group . . . the financial barons who control the world's supply of money."[12]

Professor Quigley explained central banking:

In addition to these pragmatic goals, the powers of financial capitalism had another far-reaching aim, nothing less than to create a world system of financial control in private hands able to dominate the political system of each country and the economy of the world as a whole. This system was to be controlled in a feudalist fashion by the central banks of the world acting in concert, by secret agreements arrived at in frequent private meetings and conferences. The apex of the system was to be the Bank for International Settlements in Basle, Switzerland, a private bank owned and controlled by the world's central banks which were themselves private corporations. Each central bank . . . sought to dominate its government by its ability to control Treasury loans, to manipulate foreign exchanges, to influence the level of economic activity in the country, and to influence cooperative politicians by subsequent economic rewards in the business world.[13]

That is exactly what is happening today. Central banks are trying to establish a system of global feudalism. Once you grasp the implications of that concept, you can understand why Professor Quigley's book had to be suppressed.

Are the central banks responsible for what is happening?

The Jewish Bankers

He was lord and master of the money market of the world, and of course virtually lord and master of everything else.

—Benjamin Disraeli[14]

Benjamin Disraeli became the prime minister of Great Britain in 1868, so we can assume he understood how the world financial system worked at that time. In 1844 he wrote a novel entitled *Coningsby* in which the hero of his book was told:

> **So you see, my dear Coningsby, that the world is governed by very different personages from what is imagined by those who are not behind the scenes.**[15]

Disraeli described the man who controlled the financial markets of the world:

> **Europe did require money, and Sidonia was ready to lend it to Europe. France wanted some; Austria more; Prussia a little; Russia a few millions. Sidonia could furnish them all. . . . He was lord and master of the money market of the world, and of course virtually lord and master of everything else. . . . Monarchs and ministers of all countries courted his advice and were guided by his suggestions.**[16]

Although Sidonia was only a fictional character, Nathan Rothschild controlled the financial markets of Europe in 1844 when Disraeli wrote his novel, and in those days the monarchs and the ministers of Europe courted Nathan Rothschild's advice. The Rothschilds dominated French banking during most of the nineteenth century; in the twentieth century a number of Catholic and Protestant banks challenged their influence and eclipsed their power.[17]

Those who believe that Jewish banks are responsible for our problems cite Benjamin Disraeli's book and claim that he exposed the Jewish Banking Conspiracy. Then they point to the Rothschilds, Kuhn, Loeb and Co., the Warburgs, the Lazard Bank, Lehman Brothers, and Goldman Sachs to justify their contention that Jewish bankers control the world. Although their arguments are convincing, until recently several of the world's largest banks were owned by the Japanese and, according to Professor Quigley, during the early decades of the twentieth century the three largest banks in the United States were owned by the Rockefellers, the Morgans, and the Mellons. The fourth largest bank was Kuhn, Loeb & Co., but it never controlled our banking system. Our fifth largest bank is the Bank of America. It was founded by an Italian immigrant.[18]

We are indebted to Professor Quigley for his analysis of the history of international finance. He found that the European central banks existed long before the House of Rothschild, and that powerful Catholic and Protestant banking firms have shared the European financial market with them. According to Professor Quigley, Jewish banks played an important part in financing industrial development in Europe, but they never controlled the financial institutions of the world.[19]

Alan Greenspan, chairman of the Federal Reserve Bank, is Jewish, but Paul Volker and William McChesney Martin who preceded him in that position weren't Jewish. Montague Norman controlled the Bank of England for twenty-five years,

and he was a gentile.[20] Lord Brand was the managing director of the Lazard Bank in England, and when he died Adam
Marris replaced him. Neither man was Jewish, but both men
were leaders of Rhodes' secret society.[21] Most people believe
that Lehman Brothers and Goldman Sachs are Jewish banks,
yet Pete Peterson was the CEO of Lehman Brothers before
he went to the Blackstone Group. He is Greek, and he is the
director of the Council on Foreign Relations.[22]

Dr. Dennis Cuddy discussed Goldman Sachs:

> **The huge investment banking firm of Goldman Sachs has
> included dozens of [Rhodes] scholars over the past half
> century, but never as many as in the 1990s, when at any
> given moment at least a half dozen have been partners. . . .[23]**

As strange as it may seem, many Jewish banks are controlled
by men who are not Jewish. Why did Benjamin Disraeli, who
was Jewish, write a novel about a Jewish banking conspiracy? Why do some people believe that Jews are responsible
for our problems? Because they have been deceived. The
Brotherhood has disseminated false information in an effort
to convince us that Jews are the source of our problem. Anti-
Semitism is a smokescreen created to conceal the identity of
our true enemy.

The Council on Foreign Relations

> **The most powerful clique in these elitist groups have one
> objective in common—they want to bring about the sur-
> render of the sovereignty and the national independence
> of the United States.**
>
> —Admiral Chester Ward[24]

Many well-informed people believe that the Council on Foreign Relations (CFR) is responsible for our problems. They note that prominent bankers, industrialists, politicians, media owners, and almost everyone of any importance in the United States belongs to the CFR. Since 1953 every chairman of the Federal Reserve Board, and every chairman of the Disarmament Agency have been members, as have all but one American Secretary of State, all but one Deputy Secretary of State, and all but one director of the Central Intelligence Agency. In addition, six of our last nine presidents have been CFR members.[25] What is their objective?

Admiral Chester Ward belonged to the CFR for sixteen years. In his book, *Kissinger on the Couch*, which he co-authored with Phyllis Schlafly, he wrote:

> **The most powerful clique in these elitist groups have one objective in common—they want to bring about the surrender of the sovereignty and the national independence of the United States.**[26]

Senator Barry Goldwater tried to warn the American people about the CFR in his book, *With No Apologies*. He wrote:

> **Their goal is to impose a benign stability on the quarreling family of nations through merger and consolidation. They see the elimination of national boundaries, the suppression of racial and ethnic loyalties as the most expeditious avenue to world peace.**

He then noted that CFR members control both of our political parties.

> **When we change Presidents, it is understood to mean the voters are ordering a change in national policy. Since 1945**

three different Republicans have occupied the White House. . . . Four Democrats have held this most powerful post the world has to offer. . . . With the exception of the first seven years of the Eisenhower administration, there has been no appreciable change in foreign or domestic policy direction. When a new President comes on board, there is a great turnover in personnel but no change in policy. Example: During the Nixon years Henry Kissinger, CFR member and Nelson Rockefeller's protege, was in charge of foreign policy. When Jimmy Carter was elected, Kissinger was replaced by Zbigniew Brzezinski, CFR member and David Rockefeller's protege.[27]

You would think that everyone would know of Senator Goldwater's concern, but since CFR members control almost all of our media outlets, his warning was suppressed.

Is the Council on Foreign Relations the dominant force in the world today?

The Bilderbergers

"Those who came were not the heads of states, but those who give orders to heads of states" . . . in other words, the kingmakers.

—Phyllis Schlafly[28]

Many competent researchers are convinced that the Bilderbergers rule the world. Although they acknowledge the importance of the CFR, they note that it is an American organization, and they argue that the effort to create a global government must involve people from other nations. Prince Bernhard of the Netherlands asked a group of prominent Americans and Europeans to help him determine the best way to establish a world government. The group met at the Bilderberger Hotel in Holland in 1954, and the name of the hotel where they first convened became the name of their organization. The Bilderbergers have met once or twice a year ever since.

The first edition of Phyllis Schlafly's book, *A Choice Not An Echo*, was published in May 1964. Therein she described the secretive nature of the group:

> Several years ago, the author of this book stumbled on clear evidence that very powerful men actually do meet to make plans which are kept secret from American citizens. While visiting at Sea Island, Georgia, this writer discovered the details of a secret meeting on nearby St. Simon's Island, Georgia, held at the King and Prince Hotel, February 14–18, 1957.[29]
>
> The most elaborate precautions were taken to prevent Americans from knowing who attended this secret meeting or what transpired there. . . . The participants at the St. Simon's meeting were some of the biggest names in American politics, business and the press. As described by an eye-witness observer of that meeting, "Those who came were not the heads of states, but those who give orders to heads of states"—in other words, the kingmakers. . . .
>
> Officially called DeBilderberg group, the U.S. kingmakers were joined on St. Simon's Island by a similarly select assortment of foreigners. . . . The titular head of this secret group was Prince Bernhard of the Netherlands.[30]

Why aren't the meetings of the Bilderbergers ever mentioned in the media? Because members of that organization control most of the major media outlets in the United States and Europe. Only a very powerful group can conceal its existence. Are the Bilderbergers the major force behind the effort to establish a world government?

The Trilateral Commission

> The Trilateral Commission is . . . intended to be the vehicle for multinational consolidation of the commercial and banking interests by seizing control of the political government of the United States.
>
> —Senator Barry Goldwater[31]

Everyone who has studied the effort to unite the world recognizes the importance of the Council on Foreign Relations and the Bilderbergers, but some people contend those groups are regional, and the New World Order will be established by the Trilateral Commission. They note that members of that organization control commerce and banking in the United States, Europe, and Asia, and point to Senator Barry Goldwater's warning:

> The implications in Governor Rockefeller's presentation have become concrete proposals advanced by David Rockefeller's newest international cabal, the Trilateral Commission. Whereas the Council on Foreign Relations is distinctly national in membership, the Trilateral Commission is international. Representation is allocated equally to Western Europe, Japan, and the United States. It is intended to be the vehicle for multinational consolidation of the commercial and banking interests by seizing control of the political government of the United States.[32]

Here we learn that the Trilateral Commission intends to consolidate control over "the commercial and banking interests" of the world . . . "by seizing control of the political government of the United States." That is an incredible statement. You would think that every American would be aware of it, but tragically that is not the case.

Is the Trilateral Commission behind the current effort to create a New World Order?

The Club of Rome

> A small cadre of obscure international bureaucrats are hard at work devising a system of "global governance" that is slowly gaining control over ordinary Americans' lives. Maurice Strong, a 68-year-old Canadian is the "indispensable man" at the center of this creeping UN power grab.
>
> —*National Review* magazine[33]

Some conspiracy theorists believe that European royalty are behind the current effort to unite the world. They acknowledge the importance of the groups cited, but they claim the King and Queen of Spain, and the Queen of the Netherlands are working with members of the Club of Rome to create a world government under the control of the monarchs of Europe. Some of the wealthiest and most powerful men in the world belong to the Club of Rome. In 1999, their Internet site stated that their objective is to:

> . . . Act as an international, non-official catalyst of change.[34]

The Internet site continued:

> Another new development was the decision to invite prominent world figures who share the Club's concerns to become Honorary Members. Although their positions may prevent them from taking a public stance, as in the case of the Queen of the Netherlands or the King and Queen of Spain, they can and do give valued moral support. Among the others are former President Gorbachev, former President Richard von Weizsacker of Germany, the first Presi-

dent of newly democratic Czechoslovakia, Vaclav Havel,
President Arpad Goncz of Hungary, President Carlos Me-
nem of Argentina, and the Nobel laureates Ilya Prigogine
and Lawrence Klein.[35]

Here we see European royalty working with the financial and
political leaders of the world as "an international, non–official, catalyst for change." Until recently, Maurice Strong was
listed as a member of the Club of Rome. An article in the *New
Yorker* magazine noted that:

**The survival of civilization in something like its present
form might depend significantly on the efforts of a single
man.[36]**

And an article in *National Review* magazine in September
1997 stated:

**A small cadre of obscure international bureaucrats are hard
at work devising a system of "global governance" that is
slowly gaining control over ordinary Americans' lives.
Maurice Strong, a 68-year-old Canadian, is the "indispens-
able man" at the center of this creeping UN power grab.[37]**

Who is Maurice Strong? Although he never graduated from
high school, by the time he was twenty-one he held an important position in international finance, and by the time he was
thirty-one he was the chairman of one of the largest financial
advisory companies in the world. Currently he is a senior
advisor to both Kofi Annan, the Secretary-General of the
United Nations, and James Wolfensohn, president of the World
Bank. Most people believe that Kofi Annan heads the United
Nations, but he is only a figurehead. Maurice Strong actually

runs the U.N., and he has recently reorganized its administrative structure in preparation for assuming power when the world government is established. He has been the chairman of both the Earth Council and the World Resources Institute, a co-chairman of the Council of the World Economic Forum, and a member of Toyota's International Advisory Board. He has served as president of the World Federation of the United Nations Association, as a trustee of the Aspen Institute, as director of the World Future Society, and as a director of finance of the Lindisfarne Association. He was a founding endorser of Planetary Citizens, convened the Fourth World Wilderness Congress, and served as a trustee of the Rockefeller Foundation from 1971 to 1978. He was the Secretary-General of the First Earth Summit in 1972, of the Second Earth Summit in 1992, and of the Earth Summit Plus Five in 1997.[38] The *Global Biodiversity Assessment Report* represents the concepts developed at the Second Earth Summit. It calls for the deconstruction of Western civilization, and Maurice Strong has been quoted as saying:

> **Frankly, we may get to the point where the only way of saving the world will be for industrial civilization to collapse.[39]**

According to Larry Abraham and Franklin Sanders, Maurice Strong owned a two hundred thousand-acre ranch in Colorado called "the Baca." They wrote:

> **Strong owns a large tract of land in Colorado which they call "the Baca." There Strong and his wife are establishing an international community of spiritualists, "complete with monasteries, devotees of the Vedic mother goddess, amulet-carrying native American shamans, Zen Buddhists, and**

> even Shirley MacLaine. . . . They are not only promoting a
> one-world government . . . they are also supporting a one-
> world religion to substitute for Christianity.[40]

According to an article in *West* magazine, well-known people
like Henry Kissinger, and Robert Strange McNamara have
been guests at the Baca. Robert Strange McNamara was Secretary of Defense during both the Kennedy and Johnson ad-
ministrations, and sent our soldiers to fight, bleed, suffer, and
die in Vietnam, but refused to allow them to win that war.
Why? Did it have anything to do with the new world order
and the new world religion that he and Maurice Strong seek?[41]

Mikhail Gorbachev is a communist, and Maurice Strong
is a capitalist, but both of them are associated with the Club
of Rome, and they co-authored the Earth Charter, a plan for
the civilization that lies ahead. Aren't communists and capitalists supposed to be enemies? If you study the various groups
and organizations that work behind the scenes, you will soon
discover that communists and capitalists have always worked
together because they are motivated by the same spiritual
force, and they seek the same goal.[42]

Is the Club of Rome the force behind the effort to establish a global government?

Communism

> The enormous social advances of China have benefitted
> greatly from the singleness of ideology and purpose. . . .
> The social experiment in China under Chairman Mao's
> leadership is one of the most important and successful in
> history.
>
> —David Rockefeller, 1973[43]

Did we really win the Cold War? Some people contend that
communism is still a threat because the CFR, the Bilderberg-

ers, the Trilateral Commission, and the Club of Rome are communist front organizations. They justify that belief by noting that Mikhail Gorbachev, a lifelong member of the KGB and the former dictator of the USSR, is currently working with members of the first three organizations, and is a member of a fourth, the Club of Rome.[44] They also cite Bella Dodd, who was a member of the Central Committee of the American Communist Party prior to World War II. Because she and her fellow communists were worried about how they would maintain contact with Moscow if war broke out, she asked a Soviet diplomat for instructions. She was told to contact one of three men living at the Waldorf-Astoria Hotel if they needed to know the current Communist Party line. She immediately recognized the names of all three men because they were well-known financiers. When she learned they were authorized to speak for the Soviet Union, she realized that everything she believed about communism was a lie, and that Moscow was working with Wall Street. She subsequently left the party, became a Christian, and told her story to anyone who would listen. Thomas Schuman told a similar story. He was a member of the KGB until he defected to the West. While working in Moscow he became aware of the fact that Western financiers were working closely with the leaders of the Soviet Union.[45]

Nikita Khrushchev was the dictator of the USSR, but he was deposed and sent to Siberia shortly after David Rockefeller visited the Kremlin in 1964. People who believe that capitalism and communism work together ask: "Who had the power to fire the dictator of the USSR?"[46] They also note that David Rockefeller praised Chairman Mao after returning from a trip to China in 1973. By then, Mao Tse-tung had slaughtered between forty and sixty million of his fellow countrymen, yet David Rockefeller wrote:

One is impressed immediately by the sense of national harmony. . . . There is a very real and pervasive dedication to Chairman Mao and Maoist principles. Whatever the price of the Chinese Revolution, it has obviously succeeded not only in producing more efficient and dedicated administration, but also in fostering high morale and community purpose. General social and economic progress is no less impressive. . . . The enormous social advances of China have benefitted greatly from the singleness of ideology and purpose. . . . The social experiment in China under Chairman Mao's leadership is one of the most important and successful in history.[47]

David Rockefeller viewed the Chinese revolution, and its bloody aftermath, as a successful "social experiment . . . the most important and successful in history" because it

. . . has obviously succeeded not only in producing more dedicated and efficient administration, but also in fostering high morale and community purpose.[48]

David Rockefeller was chairman of the Council on Foreign Relations for over fifteen years, a Bilderberger, and financed the formation of the Trilateral Commission.

Is it possible that communism and capitalism are working together to create a world government?

Socialism

I also made it quite clear that Socialism means equality of income or nothing, and that under Socialism you would not be allowed to be poor. You would be forcibly fed, clothed, lodged, taught, and employed whether you liked it or not. If it were discovered that you had not character

**and industry enough to be worth all this trouble, you might
possibly be executed in a kindly manner; but whilst you
were permitted to live you would have to live well.**

—George Bernard Shaw[49]

Researchers who have studied socialism realize that communism and socialism have similar goals. J. Edgar Hoover discussed the similarity between the two concepts when he wrote:

In June 1957, Nikita Khrushchev, Soviet Communist Party boss, was interviewed before a nation-wide American television audience. With calm assurance he stated: ". . . I can prophesy that your grandchildren in America will live under socialism. And please do not be afraid of that. Your grandchildren will . . . not understand how their grandparents did not understand the progressive nature of a socialist society."[50]

Nikita Khrushchev advocated socialism in the United States, not communism. Every communist works to establish socialism because they are taught that socialism is a transitional stage between capitalism and communism. There are socialist organizations in every country, and the Socialist International coordinates the worldwide socialist movement. It is one of the four most powerful groups in the world, yet most people have never heard of it.[51]

In England, the Labor Party acts as a front group for the Fabian Socialist Society which was organized in 1884 by George Bernard Shaw and his friends. Shaw explained socialism in his book, *An Intelligent Woman's Guide to Socialism and Capitalism,* but his definition is seldom mentioned today because the Socialist International doesn't want people to know what lies ahead. George Bernard Shaw wrote:

I also made it quite clear that socialism means equality of income or nothing, and that under Socialism you would not be allowed to be poor. You would be forcibly fed, clothed, lodged, taught, and employed whether you liked it or not. If it were discovered that you had not character and industry enough to be worth all this trouble, you might possibly be executed in a kindly manner; but whilst you were permitted to live you would have to live well. . . . As far as I know I was the first Socialist writer to whom it occurred to state this explicitly as a necessary postulate of permanent civilization. . . .[52]

Leaders of both major political parties support socialism, but Republican leaders pretend to oppose it.

Norman Thomas was the leader of the Socialist Party in the United States. He wrote:

The American people will never knowingly adopt Socialism, but under the name of Liberalism they will adopt every fragment of the Socialist program until one day America will be a Socialist nation without knowing how it happened.[53]

On June 9, 1966, the *Pittsburg Press* quoted Earl Browder, the former chairman of the American Communist Party, who said:

America is getting socialism on the installment plan through the programs of the welfare state. There is more real socialism in the United States today than there is in the Soviet Union.[54]

Socialists control most labor unions and use union dues to advance their legislative agenda. Despite the apparent conflict between union leaders and employers, in most cases there are secret agreements advantageous to both sides at the expense of the workers. Although socialists talk about democracy, their real goal is a world government under the control of an enlightened Elite.[55] The Socialist International coordinates its efforts with the CFR, the Trilateral Commission, the Bilderbergers, and the Club of Rome. All of them work to establish a world government. The only question is: Who will be in control?

Secular Humanism

. . . we reject those features of traditional religious morality that deny humans a full appreciation of their own potentialities and responsibilities. Traditional religions often offer solace to humans, but, as often, they inhibit humans from helping themselves. . . .[56]

Francis Schaeffer studied the decline of Western civilization, and he came to the conclusion that secular humanism is responsible for our problems because secular humanists advocate abortion, homosexuality, prisoners' rights, socialism, world government, and deny the existence of God. Every communist and every socialist is a secular humanist, and although every humanist is not a communist, every communist is a secular humanist.

The beliefs of secular humanism were codified in the second *Humanist Manifesto* where seventeen concepts were presented that changed the world. *Humanist Manifesto II* proclaimed that secular humanists:

1. Reject traditional religious beliefs, and seek "new human purposes and goals." Humanists proclaim there is "no divine purpose or providence for the human species. . . .

No deity will save us; we must save ourselves."

2. Reject as both illusory and harmful the "promises of immortal salvation or fear of eternal damnation . . ." which are the basis of both Judaic and Christian beliefs.

3. Believe that "moral values derive . . . from human experience. Ethics is autonomous and situational," and that we should "strive for the good life, here and now." Thus humanists believe that individuals determine what is right and wrong.

4. Believe that "reason and intelligence" will guide mankind to a better world.

5. Stress individual freedom without moral restraints.

6. Recognize ". . . the right to birth control, abortion, and divorce," and that ". . . the many varieties of sexual exploration should not in themselves be considered 'evil.'" Thus humanists condone homosexuality and other forms of sexual perversion.

7. Support concepts of individual freedom such as "an individual's right to die with dignity, euthanasia, and the right to suicide."

8. Advocate democracy and participatory democracy rather than a republican form of government.

9. Advocate "the separation of church and state and the separation of ideology and state." This program was designed to remove both God and prayer from public schools.

10. Advocate "alternative economic systems," and the need to "democratize the economy." Humanists promote socialism.

11. Advocate the "elimination of all discrimination based upon race, religion, sex, age, or national origin," and "the right to universal education." They also oppose "sexism or sexual chauvinism." This requires government control over every aspect of our lives.

12. Support the ending of nationhood and national sover-
    eignty, and advocate a "world community."
13. State that "this world community must renounce the re-
    sort to violence and force as a method of solving interna-
    tional disputes." They want a world government which
    includes an international court.
14. Advocated that "the world community . . . engage in co-
    operative planning concerning the use of rapidly deplet-
    ing resources . . . population growth must be checked."
    This is the basis of modern-day environmentalism and
    population control.
15. Propose foreign aid and birth control for developing na-
    tions.
16. Since "technology is a vital key to human progress . . ."
    they oppose "any moves to censor basic scientific research
    on moral, political, or social grounds."
17. Call for ". . . international cooperation in culture, sci-
    ence, the arts, and technology across ideological borders.
    We must learn to live openly together or we shall perish
    together."

Most of the concepts that are advocated in the *Humanist Manifestos I* and *II* have been implemented, and their plan to
introduce socialism, create a world government, and undermine the Judeo-Christian beliefs of our nation are well on
the way to completion. Is secular humanism the force behind unfolding world events?[57]

The Tax-Exempt Foundations

**But I felt that the work . . . left several important unan-
swered questions, of which the gravest was: to what ex-
tent, if any, are the funds of the large foundations aiding
and abetting Marxist tendencies in the United States and**

**weakening the love which every American should have for
his way of life?"**

— Congressman B. Carroll Reece[58]

Although there is a great deal of evidence to suggest that secular humanism is responsible for what is happening, their programs could never have been implemented without the support of the tax-exempt foundations. Some people believe that the great foundations are responsible for our current problems.

Following the communist takeover of China in 1950, the Senate appointed a special committee to investigate why our State Department placed an arms embargo on the Nationalist Chinese and brought Chairman Mao to power. I summarized the Senate committee's findings in chapter one. The committee also discovered that both the Rockefeller Foundation and the Ford Foundation funded communist propaganda outlets in the years preceding the fall of China. The 83rd Congress commissioned Congressman B. Carroll Reece to investigate the tax-exempt foundations to determine why they had financed communist organizations. The Reece Committee discovered:

1. In 1915 the Carnegie Endowment for International Peace launched a propaganda program to force the United States into World War I.
2. Many of our large foundations were actively promoting communism and socialism.
3. The Rockefeller Foundation financed Dr. Alfred Kinsey's badly flawed study of human sexuality, and his effort to undermine the moral standards of our nation.
4. The Rockefeller Foundation, the Carnegie Educational Foundation, and the Ford Foundation had used their

grant-making power to take over American education and force our colleges and universities to abandon their religious beliefs and moral standards.

5. The foundations influenced State Department policy and were largely responsible for bringing communism to China.[59]

6. The foundations were working to undermine our constitutional form of government.

A group of wealthy men set out to block the Reece Committee investigation. Congressman Wayne Hays was assigned to the committee to disrupt it. During one 185-minute testimony, he interrupted a total of 246 times, yet the media steadfastly refused to report what was happening.[60] The Reece Committee discovered that the tax-exempt foundations were working closely with the Rhodes Trust, and that Rhodes Scholars were being assigned to strategic positions in our government. They cited Dean Rusk as an example. After returning from Oxford University, he worked for the Rockefeller Foundation until he was appointed Undersecretary of State for Far Eastern Affairs. In that position, he helped bring communism to China and involved us in the no-win war in Korea. When he left the State Department, he returned to the Rockefeller Foundation where he remained until President Kennedy asked him to become Secretary of State. He returned to government service, and was largely responsible for our involvement in the Vietnam War. In 1968, he left the State Department and became president of the Rockefeller Foundation.[61]

Powerful men opposed the Reece Committee's effort to investigate the foundations. They brought pressure to bear on congressional leaders, and funding for the Reece Committee was cancelled, which ended the hearings. Subsequently

René Wormser, the counsel for the Reece Committee, wrote *Foundations: Their Power and Influence*. Skeptics can verify the facts about what happened there. In the foreword to René Wormser's book, Congressman B. Carroll Reece wrote:

> . . . I felt that the work . . . left several important unanswered questions, of which the gravest was: to what extent, if any, are the funds of the large foundations aiding and abetting Marxist tendencies in the United States and weakening the love which every American should have for his way of life?[62]

Are the tax-exempt foundations the force behind the effort to establish a world government?

The Hierarchy

> We affirm the fact of group fusion and integration within the heart centre of the new group of world servers, mediating between Hierarchy and humanity. . . .
>
> —letter from the Lucis Trust, 1998[63]

Some people insist that the Hierarchy are responsible for our problems. They are supposedly wise men who have evolved through successive cycles of reincarnation to reach a state of divinity; they are also called Ascended Masters, Masters of Wisdom, and The Elder Brothers.[64] Before you reject that concept, let me point out that many important people believe in the Hierarchy, and support their programs. The Lucis Trust, which has thousands of followers, promotes belief in the Hierarchy. It has offices in New York City, London, and Geneva, Switzerland. Some of the most important men in the world belong to that organization. Gary Kah lists their names in his book, *The Demonic Roots of Globalism*.[65] The fact that most people have never heard of the Lucis Trust or the Hierarchy reflects the degree of control that exists today over what the American people think.

Robert Müller belongs to the Lucis Trust and supports its objectives. He was Assistant Secretary General of the United Nations for many years, and his World Core Curriculum is currently being used in schools throughout the world to introduce students to occult thought. Alice Bailey organized the Lucis Trust in 1923 to publish and distribute her books, which were channeled to her by Djwhal Khul, her spirit guide. Her books, along with Madame Blavatsky's writings, are the foundation of New Age thought.[66]

In 1998, the Lucis Trust sent a letter to its supporters inviting them to join in—"Meditation: Letting in the Light."

At this point you may not understand the term "the Light." A clue to the meaning of that phrase can be found toward the end of their letter:

> **GROUP FUSION. We affirm the fact of group fusion and integration within the heart centre of the new group of world servers, mediating between Hierarchy and humanity. . . .**
>
> **ALIGNMENT. We project a line of lighted energy towards the spiritual Hierarchy of the planet, the planetary heart, the great Ashram of Sanat Kumara, and towards the Christ at the heart of Hierarchy.[67]**

The passage is confusing because it is written in esoteric language in order to mislead all but the Elect. Note the reference to Sanat Kumara. Who is he? What is his connection with the Hierarchy? What part does he play in the current effort to establish a world government?

The Illuminati

> . . . it was this same remembrance, preserved, or perhaps
> profaned in the celebrated Order of the Templars, that be-
> came for all the secret associations, of the Rose-Croix, of
> the Illuminati, and of the Hermetic Freemasons, the rea-
> son of their strange rites, of their signs . . . and, above all,
> of their mutual devotedness and of their power.
>
> —Albert Pike, 1871[68]

Some well-informed people believe that the Illuminati still
exists, and that it is the major force behind the drive toward
global government. Adam Weishaupt and four associates
founded the Illuminati on May 1, 1776. Their goal was to
destroy all governments, all religion, and to rule the world.
Within a few years, they recruited a number of prominent
men and began to infiltrate Masonic lodges across Europe.
There they could work under a cloak of secrecy protected by
blood oaths. Although the Illuminati was officially disbanded in 1785, it continued to exist within Freemasonry, and was
the force behind the Jacobins and the French Revolution. The
revolutionary movement of the nineteenth century culminat-
ed in the Communist Revolution in Russia and the establishment of a Bolshevik state. Why did the communists select
May 1, the day the Illuminati was founded, as their national
holiday?[69]

In 1797, the Abbe Barruel wrote *Memoirs: Illustrating the
History of Jacobinism*. In part one, volume one, "The Anti-
christian Conspiracy," he revealed that the Illuminati was the
force behind Jacobinism. In the spring of 1798, Professor John
Robison wrote *Proofs of a Conspiracy* based on his personal
knowledge of the movement.[70] On July 4, 1798, Timothy
Dwight, president of Yale University, and the grandson of
Jonathan Edwards, delivered a sermon warning the Ameri-

can people about the influence of the Illuminati, and on October 24, 1798, George Washington wrote a letter to William Russell expressing his concern about the influence of Jacobinism and the Illuminati in the United States.[71] My grandfather told my father about the secret societies, and prior to 1930 most people knew about them. Subsequently, almost all mention of them has been removed from our textbooks, encyclopedias, and reference books. As a result, most people have never heard of the Illuminati, the Jacobins, or the secret societies that fomented the bloody revolutions of the nineteenth century.[72]

During the early decades of the twentieth century, the *Encyclopaedia Britannica* included a section on the Illuminati, but modern editions seldom if ever mention it. The following information can be found in volume fourteen of the 1910 edition of the *Encyclopaedia Britannica:*

A short-lived movement of republican free thought, to whose adherents the name Illuminati was given, was founded on Mayday 1776 by Adam Weishaupt (d. 1830), professor of Canon Law at Ingolstadt, an ex-Jesuit. The chosen title of this Order or Society was Perfectibilists. Its members, pledged to obedience to their superiors, were divided into three main classes; the first including "novices," "minervals," and "lesser illuminati"; the second consisting of freemasons, "ordinary," "Scottish" and "Scottish knights"; the third or "mystery" class comprising two grades of "priest" and "regent" and of "magus" and "king." Relations with masonic lodges were established at Munich and Freising in 1780. The order had its branches in most countries of the European continent, but its total numbers never seem to have exceeded two thousand. The scheme had its attraction for literary men, such as Goethe and Herder,

**and even for the reigning dukes of Gotha and Weimar. In-
ternal rupture preceded its downfall, which was effected
by an edict of the Bavarian government in 1785. . . .[73]**

Although the Illuminati was officially disbanded in 1785,
Weishaupt's followers were firmly entrenched in Masonic
lodges by then, and blood oaths prevented other Freemasons
from revealing the dark secrets they learned. Ninety-six years
later Albert Pike, the father of modern-day Masonry, wrote:

**. . . it was this same remembrance, preserved, or perhaps
profaned in the celebrated Order of the Templars, that became for all the secret associations, of the Rose-Croix, of
the Illuminati, and of the Hermetic Freemasons, the reason of their strange rites, of their signs . . . and, above all,
of their mutual devotedness and of their power.[74]**

Researchers who have studied the secret societies claim that
the occult emblem on the back of the dollar bill represents
the Illuminati. They point to the incomplete pyramid capped
with a glorified eye and the reference to *Novus Ordo Seclorum*, the New Secular Order. They note the date at the base
of the pyramid is MDCCLXXVI which is 1776, the year the
Illuminati was formed. Why does an occult emblem appear
on the back of our dollar bill? Does it really represent the
Illuminati, or does it represent some other hidden group?

The Jews
Earlier I noted that some sincere people believe that the Jews,
or the Jewish bankers, are behind the world conspiracy. There
are many clues that lead people to that conclusion, but I can
assure you that the evidence has been planted to divert attention away from the truth. That is not to say there are no peo-

ple of Jewish extraction within the Brotherhood, but those who support that movement have renounced their belief in Judaism, and worship a different god. Anti-Semitism is a trap that has been baited to lead us away from the truth.

A number of convincing arguments are made to convince us that the Jews, or the Jewish bankers, are our enemy. The first is:

Many of the Bolsheviks were Jews, and almost all of the original members of Lenin's Politbureau were Jews.

There are several valid responses to that charge:

1. Although many of Lenin's followers were Jews, all but one of them were subsequently executed, and that's a poor way to reward Jews if they were the force behind the Bolshevik Revolution. Leon Trotsky was Jewish. He was tracked down in Mexico, and brutally murdered.
2. All but one of Jesus' original disciples were Jews, but does that make Christianity a Jewish conspiracy?
3. The third response can be found in Antony Sutton's book, *Wall Street and the Bolshevik Revolution.* He noted that many Englishmen fought on our side during the Revolutionary War, but that didn't make the Revolutionary War an English war.[75]

Another argument is that Winston Churchill exposed the Zionist plot behind Bolshevism. The response:

Although Winston Churchill did write an article in *The London Illustrated Sunday Herald* in 1920 claiming that Zionism was the force behind Bolshevism, the response from the world media was very strange. Most people who have attacked Zionism have been vilified, but Churchill always had favorable press coverage. Was that because he was part of the Brotherhood, and his article was an attempt to shift responsibility for the Russian Revolution to the Jews?[76]

Another point is made that Jacob Schiff provided $20 million to finance the Bolshevik Revolution. The following quotation can be found in the *New York Journal-American*, February 3, 1949:

> **Today it is estimated even by Jacob's grandson, John Schiff, a prominent member of New York Society, that the old man sank about $20,000,000 for the final triumph of Bolshevism in Russia. Other New York banking firms also contributed.**[77]

Those who believe that Jews, or Jewish bankers, are responsible for communism invariably refer to that quotation. Did Jacob Schiff really help the Bolsheviks? Because of the progressive dumbing-down of our people, most Americans don't realize there were two Russian revolutions. The first revolution was in March 1917 (or February if you use the old Russian calender), the second was in October of that same year. By then, World War I had been under way for three years, and almost every family had lost at least one member. The March revolution began in St. Petersburg when a contingent of military recruits refused to fire on anti-government demonstrators. When another army unit was sent to arrest them, they refused to obey their officers and joined the mutiny. Soon, almost every military unit in St. Petersburg was in revolt, and the anti-government demonstrations began to spread. In an effort to quell the uprising, the czar ordered the Duma to disband so he could assume dictatorial control. When the Duma refused, the czar was forced to abdicate. Alexander Kerensky was chosen to lead Russia until elections could be held. When it became obvious that he intended to continue the war, the German High Command approached Lenin, who was living in Switzerland. They knew he was a professional revolutionary, so they offered him money and transportation to go to Russia to overthrow Kerensky. Trotsky was living in the United States at the time. German agents sent him to Russia to help. When the two men arrived in St. Petersburg, they began building support for a counterrevolution. Initially they were financed by Germany, but after the Bolshevik Revolution, when Lenin continued the war, the Germans cut off his funds. At that point the Bolsheviks had to get money and supplies elsewhere.[78]

What part did Jacob Schiff play in fomenting the Bolshevik Revolution? During World War I, the American State Department was responsible for collecting intelligence information. Their files confirm the fact that Jacob Schiff opposed the czar, and after Kerensky took power, Jacob Schiff sent Kerensky a telegram congratulating him, but the Bolshevik Revolution didn't take place until seven months later. Antony Sutton was a Resident Scholar at the Hoover Institute for many years. When he examined the State Department's intelligence files, he found evidence that Jacob Schiff opposed the Bolsheviks and encouraged our State Department to oppose them.[79] If that is true, where did the Bolsheviks get their money after the German High Command stopped funding them?

It is impossible to understand what happened during that era unless you know about *The Protocols of the Learned Elders of Zion*. The document first appeared in Russia in 1905; it claimed that Zionists were behind the wars and revolutions of the nineteenth century, and planned to seize control of the world. Many Russians believed *The Protocols*, and they began to persecute the Jews and destroy their property. When the czar refused to intervene, Jacob Schiff began plotting to depose him. He provided revolutionary literature to the Russian soldiers captured by the Japanese during the Russo–Japanese War in 1905, and when they returned home, some of the soldiers were disillusioned with the czar's government.[80] It is even possible that some of the soldiers who participated in the March revolution read Jacob Schiff's literature, so he may have played a part in inciting the March revolution, but that was not the Bolshevik Revolution. When Antony Sutton researched the State Department intelligence files, he found documents showing that English and American financiers provided funding for the Bolsheviks, but that fact is never mentioned today. Could it be that the story of Jacob Schiff's $20 million gift to the Bolsheviks was contrived to divert attention away from the real source of their funding?[81]

The Protocols of the Learned Elders of Zion were circulated throughout Europe during the early decades of the twentieth century, and many people believed them. That led, at least in part, to the anti-Semitism that brought Adolph Hitler to power. Henry Ford circulated *The Protocols* in the United States and wrote a book entitled *The International Jew* which claimed that Jewish bankers were responsible for World War I and the Bolshevik Revolution. Henry Ford supported the Nazis, and Hitler acknowledged his support by awarding him the highest German medal available to civilians. The Ford factories in Germany provided trucks, tanks, and vehicles for Hitler's armed forces.[82] That would have been logical if Henry Ford really believed that Jewish bankers were responsible for the Bolshevik Revolution, and Hitler opposed them. The problem is that Henry Ford also built a factory complex in Russia to help the faltering communist economy. Why did Ford promote anti-Semitism in the United States, support Adolph Hitler in Germany, and support the Bolsheviks in Russia?[83]

At the present time, the Ford Motor Company has six factories in Communist China, and plans to build more. Henry Ford helped the Bolsheviks in the 1930s, and today his company is helping the Chinese communists. Why?[84]

It is impossible to understand what is happening today without understanding the origin of *The Protocols*. While going through Colonel Edward Mandell House's papers at Yale University some years ago, I came across a copy of *The Protocols of the Meeting of the Zionist Men of Wisdom*. It was essentially the same document as *The Protocols of the Learned Elders of Zion*, but the wording was different, which suggested it was a different translation of the original document.[85]

The Protocols were written in French, smuggled into Russia in 1905 where they were translated into Russian, and later transported to Great Britain where Victor Marsden translated them into English. Copies of Victor Marsden's translation are available in the United States today, but that translation is entirely different from the Colonel House version, which suggests that Colonel House's version came from another source, perhaps from the original document. Who was Colonel House, and where did he get his copy of *The Protocols?* Was he an anti-Semite?

Colonel House was able to control the men who led the world between 1912 and 1938 because he had the ability to "ooze" thoughts into their minds. Arthur Howden Smith knew him, and commented on his mystical ability:

> **Colonel House would come into an office and say a few words quietly, and after he had gone you would suddenly become seized by a good idea. You would suggest that idea to your friends or superiors and be congratulated for it; it would work first rate, beyond your wildest dreams. You might forget about it. But some time, as sure as shooting, in cogitating proudfully over it, you would come to an**

abrupt realization that that idea had been oozed into your brain by Colonel House in the course of conversation.[86]

Smith then described Colonel House's account of his third meeting with Woodrow Wilson:

> It was an evening several weeks later, when he had been paying me a . . . visit, that I said to Mr. Wilson as he rose to go: "Governor, isn't it strange that two men who never knew each other before should think so much alike?" He answered: "My dear fellow, we have known each other all our lives."[87]

By their third meeting, Woodrow Wilson was under Colonel House's control. House was well aware of his ability to control others. I found an entry in his unpublished diary where he bragged about how he convinced Premier Clemenceau of France and Premier Orlando of Italy of something he knew wasn't true. In January 1919 both men feared that the Bolsheviks intended to foment revolutions in their countries, and they wanted to send a military contingent to Russia to defeat the Bolsheviks. Colonel House wrote:

> I had a heart to heart talk with Clemenceau about Bolshevism in Russia and its westward march. I made him confess that military intervention was impossible. . . . Later in the afternoon when Orlando called, I gave him very much the same kind of talk, and he too, agreed with my conclusions. I am trying, and have partially succeeded, to frighten not only the President, but the English, French and Italians regarding what might be termed "the Russian peril." Personally, I really do not believe there is as much danger as I make it to them. . . . I would not confess that military

intervention was an impossibility because I believe that it could be successfully accomplished if gone about properly. A voluntary and a mercenary army of very small proportions, equipped with artillery and tanks, would in my opinion do the work.[88]

Here Colonel House admits that he "made" both Clemenceau and Orlando "confess" that the use of military force against the Bolsheviks would be futile, yet he knew that wasn't true. This is an example of how Colonel House was able to "ooze" ideas into the minds of the leaders of the Western world. Why did Colonel House want to protect the Bolsheviks?

James W. Gerard was the American ambassador to Germany during World War I. In his book, *My First Eighty-three Years in America*, he related another story about Colonel House. Representatives of the German government contacted Ambassador Gerard in February 1915 and asked him to notify President Wilson that they wanted to stop the war. The ambassador sent President Wilson a cable, but Colonel House replied, and told him that henceforth all communications with President Wilson were to be sent through him. Ambassador Gerard wrote:

In addition to the cable which I had already received informing me that Colonel House was "fully commissioned to act" he himself reminded me of my duty in his February 16 postcript. In his own handwriting were those words from House: "The President has just repeated to me your cablegram to him, and says he has asked you to communicate directly with me in the future. . . ." All authority, therefore, had been vested in Colonel House, and as I was directed to report to Colonel House direct, the President ceased to be even a conduit of communications.[89]

Ambassador Gerard commented on the power Colonel House had assumed:

> **He, who had never been appointed to any position, and who had never been passed upon by the Senate, was "fully instructed and commissioned" to act in the most grave situation. I have never ceased to wonder how he had managed to attain such power and influence.**[90]

Colonel House controlled President Woodrow Wilson, and the president did his bidding. Later Colonel House controlled President Roosevelt, and much of the social legislation enacted during the Roosevelt Administration involved programs that Colonel House advocated.[91] Where did Colonel House get his ability to control people's minds? I will answer that question later.

Before I go on, I must clarify the source of the funds used to finance the Russian revolutions. It is impossible to understand what is happening today without an understanding of who was responsible for the first and second Russian revolutions.

When Cecil John Rhodes died, he left his fortune to the Rhodes Trust. Lord Alfred Milner assumed control of that trust, and of Rhodes' secret society. Although he was never elected to public office, Lord Milner held many important government posts. During the first two-and-a-half years of World War I, his agents held key positions in the British government, and when Lloyd George became prime minister, Milner's men took control of England. Lloyd George recruited a staff to help him govern; four of the six members of his Secretariat were members of The Round Table, which was a front organization for the secret society that Lord Milner led.[92] On February 24, 1917, *The Nation* published an article discussing Lloyd George's Secretariat:

> . . . a little body of illuminati, whose residence is in the
> Prime Minister's garden, and their business to cultivate
> the Prime Minister's mind. These gentlemen stand in no
> sense for a Civil Service cabinet. They are rather of the
> class of travelling empirics in Empire, who came in with
> Lord Milner, and whose spiritual home is fixed somewhere
> between Balliol and Heidelberg.[93]

Lord Milner visited Russia in February 1917 shortly before
the czar was deposed. In his book *Czarism and Revolution*, A.
Goulevitch quoted responsible sources who claimed that Lord
Milner financed the March revolution.[94]

Sir George Buchanan was the English ambassador to
Russia at the time of the Revolution. In his book, *My Mission
to Moscow*, he spent sixteen pages defending himself against
charges that he and the English government were responsible for the March revolution and the death of the czar. After
World War I, that accusation was made by a number of knowl-
edgeable observers, but strangely it is never mentioned today. Why? Is it because there is a conscious effort to convince us that Jacob Schiff financed the Bolshevik Revolution?[95]

The Round Table Magazine was published by the members of Milner's secret society. Shortly after the Russian Revolution, the magazine carried an article stating that World
War I was a War of Liberation, suggesting that the end of the
monarchy in Russia had freed the people.[96]

Following the Bolshevik Revolution, Lord Milner sent
Bruce Lockhart to Russia as his personal envoy. In his book,
British Agent, R. H. Bruce Lockhart described an incident he
witnessed:

Another new acquaintance of these first days in Bolshe-
vised St. Petersburg was Raymond Robins, the head of the
American Red Cross Mission. . . . Although a rich man
himself, he was an anti-capitalist. . . . Hitherto, his two
heroes had been Roosevelt and Cecil Rhodes. Now Lenin
had captured his imagination. . . . Robins was the only man
whom Lenin was always willing to see, and who ever succeeded in imposing his own personality on the unemotion-
al Bolshevik leader. . . . I returned from my interview to
our flat only to find an urgent message from Robins re-
questing me to come to see him at once. I found him in a
state of great agitation. He had been in conflict with Saalkind, a nephew of Trotsky and then Assistant Commissar
for Foreign Affairs. Saalkind had been rude, and the American, who had a promise from Lenin that, whatever happened, a train would always be ready for him at an hour's
notice, was determined to exact an apology or to leave the
country. When I arrived he had just finished telephoning
to Lenin. He had delivered his ultimatum, and Lenin had
promised to give a reply within ten minutes. I waited, while
Robins fumed. Then the telephone rang and Robins picked
up the receiver. Lenin had capitulated. Saalkind was dis-
missed from his post. He was an old member of the Party.
Would Robins have any objection if Lenin sent him as a
Bolshevik emissary to Berne? Robins smiled grimly. "Thank
you, Mr. Lenin," he said. "As I can't send the [expletive
deleted] to hell, 'burn' is the next best thing you can do
with him."[97]

Who can give orders to the dictator of Russia? Do you remember the story about Nikita Khrushchev, the Russian dictator who was reassigned to a post in Siberia after another
prominent American visited Russia? Is it possible there is a

force that even Russian dictators must obey?

Raymond Robins represented William Boyce Thompson of the Federal Reserve Bank, Colonel House, and J. P. Morgan. Bruce Lockhart noted that he and Robins were invited to Bolshevik Executive Committee meetings, and consulted on important decisions. In his book, *The Creature from Jekyll Island*, G. Edward Griffin wrote:

> **The Bolsheviks were well aware of the power these men represented, and there was no door closed to them. They were allowed to attend meetings of the Central Executive Committee, and were consulted regarding important decisions.**[98]

Isn't it strange that an Englishman and an American were invited to attend such important meetings?

Raymond Robins worked for William Boyce Thompson who was a member of the Federal Reserve Board. When Antony Sutton researched the State Department intelligence files, he found several references to the fact that William Boyce Thompson gave Lenin $1 million. In addition, he found that Lenin nationalized every bank in Russia except the Rockefeller–controlled National City Bank, which remained open and continued to provide funds for the Bolsheviks.[99]

Where did the Bolsheviks get the food and medical supplies they needed to consolidate their control over Russia? Herbert Hoover headed the American Relief Mission following World War I. On May 28, 1919, he wrote to President Wilson:

> **As a result of the Bolshevik economic conceptions, the people of Russia are dying of hunger and disease at the rate of some hundreds of thousands monthly in a country that**

> formerly supplied food to a large part of the world. . . . The
> Bolsheviki has resorted to terror, bloodshed and murder
> to a degree long since abandoned even amongst reaction-
> ary tyrannies.[100]

At that time Lenin and his followers held only a small area;
the remainder of the country was under the control of those
who wanted to restore freedom to the Russian people. Con-
sidering the brutality and inhumanity of the Bolsheviks, you
would think that most of our relief supplies would have been
sent to the anti-communists, but that was not the case. Herbert Hoover catalogued the destination of the food and medical supplies we sent to Russia:

> **Food, clothing, and medical supplies:**
> **27,588 tons sent to the areas controlled by the anti-communists.**
> **740,571 tons sent to the areas controlled by the Bolsheviks.**
>
> **Charity from the United States:**
> **$332,508 sent to the areas controlled by the anti-communists.**
> **$55,994,588 sent to the areas controlled by the Bolsheviks.[101]**

Those figures dwarf the $20 million Jacob Schiff supposedly
sent to the Bolsheviks, yet Herbert Hoover's statistics are
never mentioned today.

In order to facilitate trade, the Bolsheviks needed an international bank. They selected several former tsarist bankers and representatives from German, Swedish, and American banks to serve on their board of directors. Funds for the
Soviet bank came from England, and the director of the Foreign Exchange division of the Bolshevik bank was Max May,
a vice president of Guaranty Trust Company, a J. P. Morgan
bank. Thus we find that British and American bankers large-

ly controlled the Bolshevik's central bank.[102]

General Wrangel led the White Russian army in southern Russia. His forces were defeating the Bolsheviks until British agents ordered him to withdraw his army to the Black Sea and leave Russia. He was told that if he refused, they would cut off his source of supplies, and his men would perish. English agents destroyed the airplanes he had purchased, and eventually General Wrangel was forced to abandon his effort to free Russia.[103]

Admiral Kolchak led the anti-communist army on the Eastern front. He, too, was defeating the Bolsheviks until his supplies were cut off by the British and American financiers who had been financing him. Once the banks had extracted the economic concessions they wanted from Lenin, they stopped supporting his enemies.[104]

In his three-volume set, *Western Technology and Soviet Economic Development*, Antony Sutton documented the fact that Russian communism has been financed by Western banks and Western corporations since its inception.[105] In his book, *Wall Street and the Bolshevik Revolution*, he documented the fact that Rockefeller and Morgan banks provided the Bolsheviks with loans, while American industry provided them with the plants and the technology they needed. Westinghouse, Henry Ford, Averill Harriman, Armand Hammer, Exxon, and other American firms built the infrastructure that allowed the Soviet Union to survive. The same thing is happening today.[106]

In 1983, John Lehman, Secretary of the Navy, told the graduating class at Annapolis:

> **Within weeks, many of you will be looking across just hundreds of feet of water at some of the most modern technology ever invented in America. Unfortunately, it is on Soviet ships.**[107]

In 1982, Senator William Armstrong addressed the United States Senate, and said:

> **America's budgetary woes would not be nearly so severe if our economy were not groaning under the strain of financing two military budgets: Our own, and a significant portion of the Soviet Union's. . . . This great irony for Americans who will be asked to tighten their belts in order to pay for our defense needs is that much of the additional money that must be spent on defense is required to offset Soviet weapons that probably could not have been built without our assistance. . . . It is difficult to overstate the extent to which the West had contributed to the military threat that now endangers our very existence.[108]**

As I noted earlier, most Jewish banks are controlled by those associated with either the Round Table or its American counterpart, the Council on Foreign Relations. Did Jacob Schiff really give the Bolsheviks $20 million? I haven't been able to document he did, but I can document the fact that the major funding for the Bolsheviks came from non-Jewish sources. There are those who would like us to believe that Zionism is the primary force behind the effort to establish a world government. It is not.

The Jesuits

Some Protestants believe that the Jesuits are behind our current problems. Ignatius Loyola organized the Society of Jesus during the sixteenth century. It was to be an army of priests dedicated to the defense of the Catholic faith and the pope. In recent years, the goal of the Order has changed, and many priests are currently promoting Liberation Theology and Marxism. Malachi Martin wrote about the tragic turn of events in his book, *The Jesuits*. The same dark spiritual forces that have permeated other religious organizations have taken over the Society of Jesus and diverted it from its original calling.[109]

Other people contend that the Knights of Malta are part of the problem. That Order was established in the twelfth century; it is also known as the Order of Saint John of Jerusalem, the Knights of the Order of the Hospital, and The Sovereign Military Jerusalemite Order of Malta. Membership is restricted to Catholics, and those who join must swear allegiance to the organization, and to the pope. Because it is one of the oldest secret societies, and because some members of the Order are working to establish a world government, there are those who contend that the Knights of Malta is an important part of the effort to establish a global government.[110]

The Masons

Some Catholics believe Protestants are responsible for what is happening. They validate their opinion by noting that many Protestants are Masons, and one of the major objectives of the Craft is the destruction of the Catholic Church. There is a good deal of evidence to substantiate their claim. Many of the men who signed our Constitution were Masons, and a Masonic architect was commissioned to design the street plan for Washington, D.C. Every federal building in our nation's Capitol bears a Masonic plaque, and five of our last eleven presidents have been Masons; a sixth was a member of the DeMolays, a Masonic club for boys. According to the book *Ten Thousand Famous Freemasons*, most of our state governors, judges, and legislators have been, or are, Freemasons. The Masonic Order controlled the United States Supreme Court between 1941 and 1971, and drastically changed our society. Four of the six Supreme Court Justices who voted to remove God and prayer from public schools were Masons:

Tom Clark, William O. Douglas, Earl Warren, and Hugo Black. Why did they do that? Because Masons worship the Great Architect of the Universe, and the goal of Masonry has always been to change our nation from a Christian country to a secular society. They have accomplished their objective.[111]

Most Masons are honest, God-fearing men, so why did the Craft destroy our Judeo-Christian heritage? In chapter one I noted that Manly P. Hall was the most distinguished Masonic philosopher of modern times. In his book *Lectures on Ancient Philosophy*, he wrote:

> **Freemasonry is a fraternity within a fraternity—an outer organization concealing an inner brotherhood of the elect . . . it is necessary to establish the existence of these two separate yet interdependent orders, the one visible and the other invisible. The visible society is a splendid camaraderie of "free and accepted" men enjoined to devote themselves to ethical, educational, fraternal, patriotic, and humanitarian concerns. The invisible society is a secret and most august fraternity whose members are dedicated to the service of a mysterious *arcanum arcanorum* (a secret or mystery). In each generation, only a few are accepted into the inner sanctuary of the work. . . .[112]**

Most Masons don't understand the purpose of the Craft. Only those who are selected to join the invisible fraternity are permitted to learn the "secret or mystery."

Paul Fisher's book, *Behind the Lodge Door*, is an excellent source of information on Freemasonry. He wrote:

> **Indeed, between 1941–1971, the Supreme Court was dominated by Masons in ratios ranging from 5 to 4 (1941–1946, 1969–1971) to 8 to 1 (1949–1956). During that 30-year-**

period, the Court erected "a wall" separating things religious from things secular. It was an epoch when prayer
and Bible reading were deracinated from public education.
. . . Masons have succeeded in having their religion dominate American society.[113]

Supreme Court Justice William O. Douglas was a Freemason. When he addressed the American Bar Association in
Louisville, Kentucky, in the 1960s, he bragged about how he
and his fellow justices had turned our Constitution on its head.
Their goal was to destroy our way of life, and they have succeeded.[114]

The New Age

Up until a few years ago the Freemasons published *The New
Age* magazine, but they changed the name of their magazine
to *The Scottish Rite Journal* when another magazine with the
same name became available. The new magazine reflected
the beliefs of the New Age. Marilyn Ferguson explained that
movement in her book, *The Aquarian Conspiracy:*

> A leaderless but powerful network is working to bring about
> radical change in the United States. Its members have bro-
> ken with certain key elements of Western thought, and they
> may even have broken continuity with history. This net-
> work is the Aquarian Conspiracy. It is a conspiracy with-
> out a political doctrine. Without a manifesto. With con-
> spirators who seek power only to disperse it, and whose
> strategies are pragmatic, even scientific, but whose per-
> spective sounds so mystical that they hesitate to discuss
> it.[115]

Marilyn Ferguson suggests that Zbigniew Brzezinski, the
former director of our National Security Council, embraces

their longing for a new spirituality. He was chosen by David Rockefeller to organize the Trilateral Commission, and that group's logo consists of three intertwined sixes, i.e. 666. It is very similar to the logo found on Marilyn Ferguson's book. The Bible tells us that 666 is the number of the Beast, the Antichrist who will one day rule the world.[116]

Thousands of world leaders embrace New Age beliefs, and their occult philosophy is gradually replacing secular humanism in our schools. New Age concepts include exploration of human sexuality, environmentalism, worship of Mother Earth, and embracing a different god.

The Order of the Quest

Some people believe that The Order of the Quest is the force behind unfolding world events. Manly P. Hall wrote about it in his book, *The Secret Destiny of America*. He noted that members of that secret group placed an unfinished pyramid on the back of the Great Seal of the United States back in 1782:

> **On the reverse of our nation's Great Seal is an unfinished pyramid to represent human society itself, imperfect and incomplete. Above floats the symbol of the esoteric orders, the radiant triangle with its all-seeing eye. . . . There is only one possible origin for these symbols, and that is the secret societies which came to this country 150 years before the Revolutionary War. . . . There can be no question that the great seal was directly inspired by these orders of the human Quest, and that it set forth the purpose for this nation. . . .[117]**

After members of The Order placed the occult emblem on the back of the Great Seal, it remained hidden there for almost one hundred fifty years until Henry Wallace convinced President Roosevelt it should be displayed on the back of the dollar bill. Both men were 32nd Degree Scottish Rite Masons, and Henry Wallace was a Theosophist. The unfinished pyramid symbolizes the fact that society is not yet complete. According to Manly P. Hall, the United States is destined to restore the legacy of Lost Atlantis, the glorious civilization Plato wrote about in his book, *The Republic*. Manly P. Hall claimed that The Order sent Adepts here shortly after the Pilgrims landed at Plymouth. Their assignment was to prepare our nation to become the *Novus Ordo Seclorum*, the secular state that one day would reconstitute Atlantis and rule the world.[118]

The Rosicrucians

Some people believe the Rosicrucians are the primary force behind world events. The Order of the Knights of the Rose-Croix is an ancient secret society. It originated with Christian Rosenkreutz, a German knight who traveled to the Near East to study Oriental magic. When he died in 1484, he transmitted his arcane knowledge to eight disciples who swore they would never reveal his secrets outside their Order. Accordingly the esoteric beliefs of the Rosicrucians have remained hidden through the centuries, although their theology is very similar to the concepts of both the Gnostics and the Kabalists. All three groups claim that the Holy Scriptures reveal only part of the truth, and to understand the Ageless Wisdom you must study their teachings.[119]

There are four Rosicrucian sects today; one of them operates the Rosicrucian Temple in San Jose, California.

Albert Pike tells us that all of the Mystery Religions pursue the Holy Word that was lost:

> . . . it was this same remembrance, preserved, or perhaps profaned in the celebrated Order of the Templars, that be-

came for all the secret associations, of the Rose-Croix, of the Illuminati, and of the Hermetic Freemasons, the reason of their strange rites, of their signs . . . and, above all, of their mutual devotedness and of their power.[120]

What was the source of the power of those groups? It was their secret knowledge.

Skull and Bones

Many people believe that Skull and Bones is the primary force that controls the world. It was organized in 1832 as Chapter 322 of a German secret society and has maintained its occult traditions by operating as a fraternity where secret oaths and bizarre customs are accepted as normal. Some people believe it was an extension of the Illuminati, although that cannot be proven. All we can be certain of is that the Illuminati continued to exist long after it was outlawed, and Adam Weishaupt died just nineteen years before Skull and Bones was chartered at Yale University. The group is known by many names. Some people call it The Order; others refer to it as The Brotherhood of Death; still others refer to it as The American Establishment. As far as we know there are no other chapters in the United States.[121]

For over one hundred and sixty-five years, prominent families have sent their sons to Yale University to become Bonesmen. Once they are inducted into the fraternity they are assured of prominent positions in life. Many become bankers, captains of industry, or politicians. All Bonesmen help their brethren to advance in society. One example is the Bush family. Prescott Bush joined Skull and Bones in 1917; his son, President George H. Bush, was selected a generation later; his grandson, Governor George W. Bush, was inducted two generations later. Only fifteen candidates are selected every year, but once they are members they become part of the ruling Elite.

Many Bonesmen have joined the Council on Foreign Relations. They are part of the small clique that controls that organization.[122]

Skull and Bones controlled the Yale newspaper so no one could criticize them. In 1873, an anonymous group formed an independent newspaper called *Iconoclast*, and wrote:

> **We speak through a new publication, because the college press is closed to those who dare to openly mention "Bones." For more than forty years a secret society called Skull and Bones has existed in Yale College. . . . By observing the men elected from year to year, we find that they are chosen with a distinct end in view, namely, that of obtaining for the society the most honors. . . . Out of every class Skull and Bones takes its men. They have gone out into the world and have become, in many instances, leaders in society. They have obtained control of Yale. . . . Year by year the deadly evil is growing. . . .[123]**

Nothing has changed. The Whitney family, the Phelps family, the Bundy family, the Lord family, the Rockefeller family, the Harriman family, the Weyerhaeuser family, the Perkins family, the Stimson family, the Taft family, the Wadsworth family, the Gilman family, the Payne family, the Davison family, the Pillsbury family, the Bush family, and the Sloane family have all had family members inducted into Skull and Bones. Many Bonesmen belong to the small clique that covertly rules the world.[124]

The Theosophical Society

Others believe that Theosophy is the hidden force that rules the world. Helena Petrovna Blavatsky organized the Theo-

sophical Society in 1875. Although she had little formal education, she wrote two books that changed the world. Both
The Secret Doctrine and *Isis Unveiled* were channeled to her
by Koot Hoomi, a spiritual master she met in India. Many
prominent people became Theosophists after reading her
books. Arthur Conan Doyle, who created Sherlock Holmes,
was a Theosophist, as was William Stead, the man who helped
Cecil Rhodes organize his secret society. Thomas Edison was
one of Madame Blavatsky's most famous disciples. By following her teachings, he learned to meditate, and during his
periods of contemplation he accessed the occult power she
promoted. That was the source of his genius and the force
behind his amazing career. Because of his dedication to Madame Blavatsky's teaching he changed the world in which
we live.[125]

The Theosophical Society exists today. It has libraries in
both Wheaton, Illinois, and Ojai, California. Every year, thousands of people join together to pray for the knowledge and
understanding that comes from the Ageless Wisdom.[126]

Corrine McLaughlin and Gordon Davidson co-authored
the book *Spiritual Politics*, in which they discussed Madame
Blavatsky's influence on Western culture:

> Over the last hundred years, the Ageless Wisdom has spread
> widely in the West, beginning with the work of the Rus-
> sian Helena Petrovna Blavatsky. Her seminal book, *The
> Secret Doctrine*, published in 1888, synthesized Christian,
> Jewish, and Islamic mysticism with the Eastern teachings
> of Hinduism, Taoism, and Buddhism, showing their com-
> mon roots and comparing their sacred texts. During her
> extensive travels in the East, Blavatsky worked directly with
> several Indian and Tibetan masters who helped her record
> and explain the Ageless Wisdom for the West.[127]

The origin of the New Age Movement, environmentalism, Christian apostasy, and modern-day occultism can be traced back to Madame Blavatsky and Theosophy.

Have you ever wondered how Adolph Hitler seized power in Germany, or why he and his henchmen slaughtered millions of helpless human beings? Almost everyone has heard of the six million Jews who perished during the Holocaust, but very few people have heard of the twelve million others who were killed in Hitler's death camps. How can we explain such barbarity, and the fact that knowledge of the deaths of the twelve million "others" has been suppressed?[128]

Adolph Hitler read Madame Blavatsky's book, *The Secret Doctrine,* nightly. That was the source of his power and his ability to control others. After the war, Winston Churchill suppressed efforts to expose Adolph Hitler's occultism. Why?[129]

Corrine McLaughlin and Gordon Davidson wrote:

Winston Churchill reportedly insisted that the black magic of the Nazi party not be revealed to the general public after the war, and the Allied prosecution and judges at Nuremberg consciously ignored the occult aspects of the Nazis' tremendous power and cruelty.[130]

Margaret Sanger was a Theosophist, and her eugenic policies and birth control programs were products of her occult beliefs.[131]

Henry Wallace was a Theosophist. He convinced President Roosevelt that the occult emblem on the back of the Great Seal of the United States should be printed on the back of the dollar bill. He later ran for president with the support of the Communist Party.[132]

Is it possible that Theosophy is the hidden force behind world events?

UFO Believers

Thousands of people claim they have seen Unidentified Flying Objects, and millions of people believe the government is covering up the truth about them. My wife insists that she and her father watched a UFO hover over a lake in front of them many years ago, and Chuck Missler wrote an excellent book on alien abductions. There are dozens of support groups for people who claim they have been kidnapped by aliens. Reports of crop circles and cattle mutilations from across the world suggest that there are supernatural forces we don't understand. Some people are convinced that the UFOs are responsible for everything that is going on in the world, and some responsible researchers believe there is an element of truth to that belief. Do UFOs really exist? Are they somehow related to the unfolding of world events?[133]

A number of strange concepts have been covered in this chapter. How does all of the information presented fit together? You are about to learn the *arcanorum*, the secret of the esoteric societies that has been hidden from public view since time began.

Footnotes

1. Barry Goldwater, *With No Apologies*, William Morrow and Company Inc., New York, 1979, p. 280.
2. Edward Hunter, *Brainwashing: The Story of Men Who Defied It*, Pyramid Books, New York, 1958, pp. 18–40.
3. Carroll Quigley, *Tragedy and Hope: A History of the World in Our Time*, The Macmillan Company, New York, 1966, p. 325.
4. Benjamin S. Catchings, *Master Thoughts of Thomas Jefferson*, The Nation Press, New York, 1907, p. 169.
5. Facts on File: Text of Governor Bill Clinton's Speech Accepting the Democratic Presidential Nomination, July

16, 1992, p. 519.E.

6. Audio copies of the interview with Professor Quigley are available by calling 800-544-8927.

7. Carroll Quigley, op cit., p. 325.

8. *Colonel House's Papers*, Sterling Library, Yale University. Quoted in Dennis Cuddy, *Secret Records Revealed*, Hearthstone Publishing, Oklahoma City, 1999, p. 53.

9. *Congressional Record*, Second Session, Sixty-Fourth Congress, Volume LIV, p. 2947-48. Reprinted in "The Sustainable Development Syllabus," available at 800-544-8927.

10. Carroll Quigley, op cit., p. 324.

11. Dennis Cuddy, op cit., p. 5.

12. Ibid., p. 5.

13. Carroll Quigley, op cit., p. 324.

14. Benjamin Disraeli, *Coningsby*, Alfred A. Knopf, originally published in England in 1844, New York, p. 225. Quoted in G. Edward Griffin, *The Creature from Jekyll Island*, American Media, Westlake Village, California, 1998, p. 228.

15. Dennis Cuddy, op cit., p. 206.

16. Disraeli, op cit., p. 225.

17. Quigley, op cit., pp. 50, 62, 77, 519–29.

18. Ibid., pp. 529–35.

19. Ibid., pp. 50–62.

20. Ibid., p. 62.

21. Ibid., p. 950.

22. Peter G. Peterson, *Facing Up*, Simon and Schuster, New York, 1993, p. 13.

23. Cuddy, op cit., p. 11.

24. Goldwater, op cit., p. 278.

25. Robert Gaylon Ross, *Who's Who of the Elite*, RIE, H.C.R. 1, Box 516 Spicewood, Texas 78669-9549

26. Goldwater, op cit., p. 278. Quoted from, *Kissinger on the Couch* by Admiral Chester Ward and Phyllis Schlafly.

27. Ibid., pp. 277–78.

28. Phyllis Schlafly, *A Choice Not An Echo*, Pere Marquette Press, 1964, p. 105.

29. Ibid., p. 103.

30. Ibid., p. 103–05.

31. Goldwater, op cit., p. 280.

32. Ibid.

33. Ronald Bailey, "Who Is Maurice Strong?", *National Review*, September 1, 1997, p. 32.

34. Club of Rome web site, June 1999: *www.clubofrome.org/hist/ho7.htm*.

35. Ibid.

36. Ronald Bailey, op cit., p. 32.

37. Ibid.

38. Larry Abraham and Franklin Sanders, *The Greening*, Soundview Publications, 1993, pp. 99–102.

39. Ronald Bailey, op cit. p. 34.

40. Larry Abraham et al, op cit., p. 100.

41. Daniel Wood, "The Wizard of Baca Grande," *West Magazine*, May 1990, p. 43.

42. Henry Lamb, "Earth Charter: analysis and comment," *Ecologic*, Hollow Rock, Tennessee, May/June 1997, p. 12.

43. Dennis Cuddy, op cit., p. 117.

44. The Club of Rome web site, June 2000, *www.clubofrome.org/flash/organisation/members/honorary.htm*

45. Robert Goldsborough, Radio Liberty interview, December 28, 1999.

46. Gary Allen, *None Dare Call It Conspiracy*, Concord Press, Rossmoor, California, 1972, p. 107.

47. Cuddy, op cit., p. 117–18.

48. Ibid.

49. George Bernard Shaw, *An Intelligent Woman's Guide to Socialism and Capitalism*, p. 470.

50. J. Edgar Hoover, *Masters of Deceit*, Holt, Rinehart and Winston, New York, 1958, p. 3.

51. Rose L. Martin, *Fabian Freeway*, Western Islands, Boston, pp. 376–79.

52. George Bernard Shaw, op cit., p. 470.

53. Cuddy, op cit., p. 41.

54. Jerry Klein, "Earl Browder, Twice Candidate for President, Now Lives Quietly," *The Pittsburg Press*, June 19, 1966, Sec. 1, p 11.

55. Golda Meir, *My Life*, G. P. Putnam's Sons, New York, 1975, p. 154.

56. Paul Kurtz, *Humanist Manifestos I* and *II*, Prometheus Books, New York, 1973, p. 16.

57. Paul Kurtz, op cit., pp. 13–23.

58. René Wormser, *Foundations: Their Power and Influence*, Devin-Adair, New York, 1958, pp. v–vi. Reprinted by Radio Liberty. Available at 800-544-8927.

59. Ibid., pp. 45–47.

60. Ibid., p. 366.

61. Ibid., p. 202.

62. Ibid., pp. v–vi.

63. Letter from the Lucis Trust, June 9, 1998.

64. Gary Kah, *The Demonic Roots of Globalism*, Huntington House, Lafayette, Louisiana, 1995, pp. 31–40.

65. Ibid., p. 28.

66. Ibid., pp. 28–29.

67. Lucis Trust Letter, op cit.

68. Albert Pike, *Morals and Dogma of the Ancient and Accepted Scottish Rite of Freemasonry*, Washington, D.C., 1960. (Originally published in 1871), p. 840.

69. James H. Billington, *Fire in the Minds of Men*, Basic Books, Inc., New York, 1980, pp. 93–99.

70. The Abbe Barruel, *Memoirs, Illustrating the History of Jacobinism*, T. Burton and Company, London, 1797. See Also: John Robison, *Proofs of a Conspiracy*. Originally printed in 1798: reprinted by Western Islands, and available at 800-544-8927.

71. John C. Fitzpatrick, editor, "The Writings of George Washington 1745–1799," volume 36, letter to George Washington Snyder, October 24, 1798. Available from the Library of Congress. See Also: Timothy Dwight, *The Duty of Americans, At the present Crisis, Illustrated in a Discourse, Preached on the Fourth of July, 1798*, Thomas and Samuel Green, 1798, pp. 1367–94.

72. James H. Billington, op cit., pp. 3–10.

73. *Encyclopaedia Britannica*, New York, 1910, Volume XIV.

74. Albert Pike, op cit., p. 840.

75. Antony C. Sutton, *Wall Street and the Bolshevik Revolution*, Arlington House, 1974, pp. 185–189.

76. Ibid.

77. Dennis Cuddy, op cit., p. 77.

78. Quigley, op cit., pp. 385–88. See Also: Radio Liberty interview, Jeff Nyquist, June 6, 2000.

79. Sutton, op cit., p. 189.

80. Naomi Wiener Cohen, *Jacob H. Schiff: A Study in American Jewish Leadership*, Brandeis Press, December 1999.

81. Sutton, op cit, p. 189.

82. Antony C. Sutton, *Wall Street and the Rise of Hitler*, '76 Press, Seal Beach, California, pp. 89–97.

83. Antony C. Sutton, *National Suicide: Military Aid to the Soviet Union*, Arlington House, New Rochelle, New York, pp. 124–26.

84. Ibid.

85. Colonel House's Papers, op cit, copy of *The Protocols*.

86. Arthur D. Howden Smith, *The Real Colonel House*, George H. Doran Co, New York, 1918, pp. 120–21.

87. Ibid., pp. 94–5.

88. Colonel House's Diary, Yale University, January, 1919. See Also: Cuddy, op cit., pp. 34–35.

89. James W. Gerard, *My First Eighty-three Years in America*, Doubleday & Company, Inc, 1951, p. 229.

90. Ibid, p. 230.

91. Ibid.

92. John Turner, *Lloyd George's Secretariat*, Cambridge University Press, 1949, p. 2. Here we find the names of the members of the Secretariat. Index read *Tragedy and Hope*, and you find that four of the six members belonged to the Round Table.

93. Ibid., p. 1.

94. A. Goulevitch, *Czarism and Revolution*, translated from the French by N. J. Couriss, Omni Press.

95. Sir George Buchanan, *My Mission to Russia and Other Diplomatic Memories*, Little, Brown and Co., 1923, pp. 90–106.

96. *A War of Liberation*, The Round Table Magazine, 1918, p. 409.

97. R. H. Bruce Lockhart, *British Agent*, G. Putnam's Sons, New York and London, 1933, pp. 225–26. See Also: G. Edward Griffin, *The Creature from Jekyll Island*, Western Islands, 1995, p. 282.

98. Ibid.

99. Sutton, *Wall Street and the Bolshevik Revolution*, op cit., pp. 75–91, 95–96, 100–101, 105.

100. Herbert Hoover, *The Memoirs of Herbert Hoover: Years of Adventure 1874–1920*, The Macmillian Company, New York, 1952, p. 413.

101. Ibid., p. 420.

102. Sutton, *Wall Street and the Bolshevik Revolution*, pp. 170–78.

103. General Wrangel, *The Memoirs of General Wrangel*, Duffield & Co., 1930, pp. 209, 279.

104. Sutton, *Wall Street and the Bolshevik Revolution*, pp. 102, 146, 166–67.

105. Antony C. Sutton, *Western Technology and Soviet Economic Development*, Three Volume Set, The Hoover Institution.

106. Sutton, *Wall Street and The Bolshevik Revolution*, pp. 15–19, 26–54, 76, 117, 183.

107. G. Edward Griffin, op cit., p. 303.

108. Ibid., p. 304.

109. Malachi Martin, *The Keys of This Blood*, Simon and Schuster, 1990, p. 261. Also, *The Jesuits* and *Windswept House*.

110. St. John of Jerusalem, *Encyclopedia Americana*, International Edition, Americana Corporation, New York, 1966, Volume 24, p. 134.

111. Paul Fisher, *Behind the Lodge Door*, Tan Books and Publishers, Inc., Rockford, Illinois, p. 244.

112. Manly P. Hall, *Lectures on Ancient Philosophy*, Philosophical Research Society, Inc., 1984, p. 433.

113. Fisher, op cit.

114. Radio Liberty Interview, April 11, 2000, 4:00–5:00 p.m.

115. Marilyn Ferguson, *The Aquarian Conspiracy*, J. P. Tarcher, Inc., Los Angeles, and Thomas Nelson and Sons, Ltd., Ontario, Canada, 1980, p. 23.

116. Ibid,, p. 363.

117. Manly P. Hall, *The Secret Destiny of America*, Philosophical Research Society, Inc., pp. 174, 181.

118. Corrine McLaughlin and Gordon Davidson, *Spiritual*

Politics, Ballantine Books, New York, 1994, p. 249.

119. *Encyclopedia Americana*, op cit. Volume 23, p. 701.

120. Albert Pike, op cit, p. 840.

121. Antony C. Sutton, *America's Secret Establishment*, Liberty House Press, Billings, Montana, 1986, pp. 5–10.

122. Ibid., p. 36.

123. Ibid., pp. 11–14.

124. Ibid., pp. 19, 29, 121.

125. Corrine McLaughlin, op cit., pp. 15–16.

126. *Encyclopedia Americana*, op cit., Volume 26, pp. 523–526.

127. Corrine McLaughlin, op cit., pp. 15–16.

128. Norman Cohn, *Warrant for Genocide*, Harper and Rowe, 1966, p. 15.

129. Debra Rae, *The ABCs of Globalism*, Huntington House, 1999, p. 82. See Also: McLaughlin, op cit., pp. 261–62.

130. Ibid. pp. 260–61.

131. George Grant, *Killer Angel*, Ars Vitae Press, New York, p. 90.

132. McLaughlin, op cit. p. 249.

133. Paul Christopher, *Alien Intervention*, Huntington House, Lafayette, Louisiana, 1998.

Chapter Three

the murder on the orient express

Why should we not form a secret society with but one object the furtherance of the British Empire, for the bringing of the whole uncivilized world under British rule. . . .

—Cecil John Rhodes, 1877[1]

At this point we must return to our story of *The Murder on the Orient Express.* Inspector Poirot realized that someone had altered the crime scene to confuse him. Then he found a piece of burned paper with the two words written on it, "Daisy" and "Arms." At that point, he began to wonder if Mr. Ratchet's murder was related to the murder of Daisy Armstrong. Daisy was a beautiful little girl who lived with her parents in New England until she was abducted by two men. The kidnappers assured Daisy's parents they would return their daughter if the ransom was paid, but when they got the money, they murdered Daisy and fled. One of them was apprehended, tried, and sentenced to death. Shortly before he was executed, the condemned man revealed that his accomplice was a man named Crosetti, but Crosetti was never found.

Daisy's mother was overcome with grief and died while giving birth to a stillborn child. The police suspected the Armstrong's maid was involved in the kidnapping, and they questioned her repeatedly. Although the young woman was innocent, she became despondent, jumped from a window, and died. Daisy's father, Colonel Armstrong, was a retired army officer. Faced with four tragic deaths, he took his own life, so there were five deaths associated with Daisy Armstrong's murder. When Inspector Poirot assembled the evidence, he noted that everything pointed to the fact that Mr. Ratchet was the second kidnapper, Crosetti, and when he questioned the passengers he found that several of them had known the Armstrongs. One was Mrs. Armstrong's godmother, another had been the Armstrong's cook. The family's chauffeur was there, as was the father of the girl who committed suicide. Could that have happened by accident? New clues kept appearing, and it soon became apparent that they were all designed to conceal the identity of the person, or persons, who had murdered Crosetti.

In many ways we face the same dilemma today. How can we possibly determine who is responsible for our problems when there are so many clues and so many suspects?

At this point I must tell you how I came to write this story. In the early 1960s I was a busy young orthopedic surgeon, and like most people, I was unconcerned about what was going on in the world. Then someone told me that our State Department brought Fidel Castro to power despite the fact they knew he was a communist. I couldn't believe that was true, but after reading the *Senate Report* on the fall of Cuba, it was obvious that someone in our State Department had betrayed the Cuban people.[2] At that point, I realized that something was seriously wrong, and I set out to determine who was responsible for establishing a communist bastion ninety miles from our Florida Keys.

I began to read and study. Initially I read about the Bolsheviks, and how they murdered sixty million people after coming to power.[3] Then I learned about the millions of women who were raped in Eastern Europe after World War II, and how we financed the Soviet occupation forces that carried out that atrocity.[4] Elsewhere, I read about the forty to eighty million Chinese who were butchered after our State Department brought Chairman Mao to power, and the fifteen to twenty thousand American soldiers who were abandoned by our government and allowed to perish in Siberian prison camps following World War II.[5, 6] Then I read about Operation Keelhaul. It involved the forced repatriation of five to six million Russians and Cossacks who were held in Western nations at the end of World War II. Many of them committed suicide rather than return to their homeland, and most of those sent back were either executed or sent to Siberia to die working in slave labor camps.[7] I wondered why I hadn't learned about those things when I attended the University of California as an undergraduate student, and why I hadn't read about them in some news magazine. At that point I began to suspect that someone, or some group, was censoring our news, and that realization motivated me to continue my search for the truth.[8]

In 1962 the communists controlled Russia, all of eastern Europe, half of Germany, North Korea, China, Cuba, North Vietnam, Laos, and Indonesia. In addition, Syria, Algeria, Iraq, Libya, India, Egypt, Burma, several South American nations, and several African nations were Soviet client states.[9] The American people should have been concerned about what was happening, but they weren't.

In 1963 I read René Wormser's book, *Foundations: Their Power and Influence*. It was the story of a congressional committee that was asked to evaluate the tax-exempt foundations to determine what they were doing with their funds. Congressman B. Carroll Reece of Tennessee led the committee, and despite repeated efforts to block his investigation, he discovered that the Ford Foundation, the Rockefeller Foundation, and the Carnegie Foundation were using their grant-making power to finance communist organizations, and destroy the love every American should have for his way of life.[10] That didn't make sense. Why were the tax-exempt foundations trying to destroy our nation?

Then I read Dan Smoot's book, *The Invisible Government.* It described the Council on Foreign Relations and how it interlocked with the tax-exempt foundations, the State Department, and the leaders of both political parties. In those days the CFR was the most powerful organization in the United States, yet most people had never heard of it.[11]

In 1964, I read Phyllis Schlafly's book, *A Choice Not an Echo,* which introduced me to the Bilderbergers, and later I learned about the Trilateral Commission and the Club of Rome. When I studied those groups, I discovered they were committed to forcing the United States to accept the rule of the United Nations, and they were working closely with the communists.[12] The more I learned, the more confused I became. Why were people of great wealth working with our enemies?

In 1966, I read *Tragedy and Hope: A History of the World in Our Time* and found answers to some of my questions. Professor Quigley assured his readers that the threat of communism was exaggerated, and that he had researched the men and the organizations that rule the world. In those days, many people believed that our State Department had turned Eastern Europe and China over to the communists because our government was dominated by subversive agents. Professor

Quigley ridiculed that idea:

> This myth, like all fables, does in fact have a modicum of
> truth. There does exist, and has existed for a generation,
> an international Anglophile network which operates, to
> some extent, in the way the radical Right believes the Com-
> munists act. In fact, this network, which we may identify
> as the Round Table Groups, has no aversion to cooperat-
> ing with the Communists, or any other groups, and fre-
> quently does so. I know of the operations of this network
> because I have studied it for twenty years, and was permit-
> ted for two years, in the early 1960s, to examine its papers
> and secret records.[13]

Professor Quigley explained the movement that initially created the Round Table Groups, and later organized the Council on Foreign Relations:

> Until 1870 there was no professorship of fine arts at Ox-
> ford, but in that year . . . John Ruskin was named to such
> a chair. He hit Oxford like an earthquake, not so much
> because he talked about fine arts, but because he talked
> also about the empire and England's downtrodden mass-
> es, and above all because he talked about all three of these
> things as moral issues. . . . Ruskin's message had a sensa-
> tional impact. His inaugural lecture was copied out in long-
> hand by one undergraduate, Cecil Rhodes, who kept it with
> him for thirty years.[14]

Professor Ruskin advocated uniting the world under the English monarchy, and extending British culture to the people
of the world. Cecil Rhodes was fascinated with John Ruskin's
concept, and he set out to acquire control of the diamond
and gold mines of southern Africa so he could use his wealth

to implement Ruskin's vision. At a relatively young age Cecil Rhodes became one of the wealthiest men in the world, and in 1877 he wrote his *Confession of Faith*. There he laid out a plan to form a secret society to bring the entire world under British rule. He wrote:

> **Why should we not form a secret society with but one object the furtherance of the British Empire for the bringing of the whole uncivilized world under British rule. . . .**[15]

Professor Quigley tells us that Cecil Rhodes organized a secret society sixteen years later, in February 1891. His first three recruits were William T. Stead, Lord Alfred Milner, and a man named Brett, who later became Lord Esher.[16] Rhodes then set out to force the Boer Republics to join the British-held Cape Colony as the first step toward uniting the world. He tried to precipitate a rebellion in Johannesburg in 1895, and when that effort failed, he and his fellow conspirators plotted to create the Boer War.[17] William T. Stead was a well-known writer; he used his contacts in the English press to promote the Boer War. Lord Milner was appointed British High Commissioner in South Africa; he precipitated the Boer War. Brett became the chief political advisor to the English monarchy; he convinced both Queen Victoria and King Edward II they should support the Boer War.[18] It was a costly undertaking. The Boers lost seven thousand men; the English army had one hundred thousand casualties.[19] Lord Milner ordered the British army to implement a scorched-earth policy to force the Boers to surrender, and when the war ended, the Transvaal lay in ruins. Cecil Rhodes died in 1902, and Lord Milner assumed control of Rhodes' Trust and his secret society. Like Rhodes, Milner believed in John Ruskin's vision of uniting the world under British rule. Accordingly, he brought a group of young aristocrats to South Africa to help rebuild the Transvaal, and while they were there he taught them about their obligation to help others, and about Rhodes' plan to unite the world. The group came to be known as "Milner's Kindergarten," and eventually became the outer circle of his secret society. In 1909, the Kindergarten returned to England and organized the first Round Table Group. Subsequently Round Table Groups were formed in other nations to pursue world government.[20]

Professor Quigley tells us:

> **The Round Table Groups were semi-secret discussion and lobbying groups organized . . . on behalf of Lord Milner, the dominant Trustee of the Rhodes Trust. . . . The original purpose of these groups was to seek to federate the English-speaking world along lines laid down by Cecil Rhodes . . . and William T. Stead . . . and the money for the organizational work came originally from the Rhodes trust. By 1915 Round Table Groups existed in seven countries, including England . . . (and) the United States. . . . Since 1925 there have been substantial contributions from wealthy individuals, and from foundations and firms associated with the international banking fraternity, especially . . . organizations associated with J. P. Morgan, the Rockefeller and Whitney families, and the associates of Lazard Brothers and of Morgan, Grenfell, and Company.**[21]

Thus we see the close relationship that developed between the Round Table Groups and the international banking fraternity. Lord Milner, members of his Round Table Groups, and several of Professor Ruskin's other disciples gained control of the English government, fomented World War I, and forced Great Britain into that war. Why? To create the League of Nations and a world government.[22] When the war ended, England was bankrupt. Lord Milner's men met with Colonel

House and his followers at the Paris Peace Conference and asked them to take over leadership of their movement. The Americans agreed. As a result of the meetings that followed, Royal Institutes of International Affairs were established in several of the Commonwealth nations, and the Council on Foreign Relations was created in the United States.[23]

Professor Quigley tells us that Lionel Curtis, a member of Milner's Kindergarten, was assigned the task of creating the new organizations:

> At the end of the war of 1914, it became clear that the organization of this system had to be greatly extended . . . the task was entrusted to Lionel Curtis who established, in England and each dominion, a front organization to the existing local Round Table Group. This front organization, called the Royal Institute of International Affairs, had as its nucleus in each area the existing submerged Round Table Group. In New York it was known as the Council on Foreign Relations, and was a front for J. P. Morgan and Company in association with the very small American Round Table Group. . . . In fact, the original plans for the Royal Institute of International Affairs and the Council on Foreign Relations were drawn up at Paris.[24]

On page 866 of his book, Professor Quigley revealed what lies ahead, and the fraudulent nature of our political process:

> . . . it is increasingly clear that, in the twentieth century, the expert will replace the industrial tycoon in control of the economic system even as he will replace the democratic voter in control of the political system. . . . Hopefully, the elements of choice and freedom may survive for the ordinary individual in that he may be free to make a choice between two opposing political groups (even if these groups

have little policy choice within the parameters of policy established by the experts) and he may have the choice to switch his economic support from one large unit to another. But, in general, his freedom and choice will be controlled within very narrow alternatives by the fact that he will be numbered from birth and followed, as a number, through his educational training, his required military or other public service, his tax contributions, his health and medical requirements, and his final retirement and death benefits.[25]

He then explained how our electoral process really works:

The chief problem of American political life for a long time has been how to make the two Congressional parties more national and international. The argument that the two parties should represent opposed ideals and policies, one, perhaps, of the Right and the other of the Left, is a foolish idea acceptable only to doctrinaire and academic thinkers. Instead, the two parties should be almost identical, so that the American people can "throw the rascals out" at any election without leading to any profound or extensive shifts in policy.[26]

Have you ever wondered why we don't try to win the wars we send our men to fight? Professor Quigley explained the new agenda:

The rather naive American idea that war aims involve the destruction of the enemy's regime, and the imposition on the defeated people of a democratic system with a prosperous economy . . . will undoubtedly be replaced by the idea that the enemy regime must be maintained, perhaps in a modified form, so that we have some government with

whom we can negotiate in order to obtain our more limited aims.[27]

Most people believe that Hitler took over the Rhineland, Austria, and the Sudetenland because of Prime Minister Chamberlain's policy of appeasement, but that wasn't the case. Professor Quigley tells us that the Round Table Group supported Adolph Hitler and encouraged him to take Austria and the Sudetenland.[28] It is impossible to understand the events that led up to World War II unless you know about Cecil Rhodes' secret society, and realize that it dominated the British government during that era.[29]

One of Professor Quigley's most shocking revelations was the fact that the American Communist Party was partly financed by J. P Morgan and Company.[30]

The chief evidence, however, can be found in the files of the HUAC (House Un-American Activities Committee) which show Tom Lamont [a senior partner in J. P. Morgan and Company—Ed.], his wife Flora, and his son Corliss as sponsors and financial angels to almost a score of extreme Left organizations, including the Communist Party itself.[31]

The American people have been led to believe the communists are our enemy, but Professor Quigley suggested that was not the case:

The two ends of this English-speaking axis have sometimes been called, perhaps facetiously, the English and American Establishments. There is, however, a considerable degree of truth behind the joke, a truth which reflects a very real power structure. It is this power structure which the Radical Right in the United States has been attacking for years in the belief that they are attacking the Communists.

This is particularly true when these attacks are directed, as they so frequently are at "Harvard Socialism," or at "Left-wing newspapers" like the *New York Times* and the *Washington Post*, or at foundations and their dependent establishments.[32]

Professor Quigley noted that during the first half of the twentieth century J. P. Morgan and his associates financed the Republican Party, the Democratic Party, conservative groups, liberal organizations, communist groups, and anti-communist organizations.[33] Thus we should not be surprised to learn that someone purchased Professor Quigley's publisher and destroyed the plates to the first half of his book so it couldn't be reprinted.[34]

In 1972, I read *None Dare Call It Conspiracy*. The authors utilized a great deal of Professor Quigley's information, but they disagreed with his conclusions. They believed communism was controlled from the United States, and pointed to the fact that Nikita Khruschev, the most powerful man in the USSR, was deposed and sent to Siberia shortly after David Rockefeller visited Russia in 1964. They asked: "Who has the power to fire the man who was supposedly the absolute dictator?"[35]

Another important source of information was Antony Sutton's book, *Wall Street and the Rise of Hitler* (1975). There I learned that General Motors, General Electric, International Telephone and Telegraph Company, the Ford Motor Company, Chase Manhattan Bank, the Guaranty Trust Company (a Morgan bank), Exxon, and many other American corporations, financed Adolph Hitler and provided him with the weapons and supplies he needed to wage World War II.[36]

When I went through Colonel House's papers at Yale University, I found a letter William E. Dodd sent to Colonel House.

Dodd was our ambassador to Germany in 1936, and he wanted to know why American corporations were building weapons for Adolph Hitler when they couldn't get their profits out of Germany because of the exchange controls.[37]

Antony Sutton's three-volume treatise, *Western Technology and Soviet Economic Development,* revealed that our banks and our corporations provided the Bolsheviks with the technology and money they needed to control the Russian people.[38] In chapter two I noted that the American Relief Mission provided the Bolsheviks with the food and medical supplies they needed to consolidate their control after World War I.[39]

One of the most disturbing books I read was *National Suicide.* There Antony Sutton documented the fact that we financed the Soviet Union during the Vietnam era, which allowed them to finance the North Vietnamese war effort. Over eighty percent of the weapons that were used to kill and cripple our men in southeast Asia came from Russia, and by the time the war ended we and our allies had loaned the USSR and its Eastern European satellites over $40 billion.[40] Later, many of those loans were written off. Unless we can convince the American people that we have financed communism since its inception, the sacrifice of those who died in the rice paddies of South Vietnam will have been meaningless, and their lives will have been lost in vain.[41]

Footnotes

1. Cecil Rhodes' *Confession of Faith,* Rhodes House, Oxford University, England. Also available from Radio Liberty, P.O. Box 13, Santa Cruz, California 95063.

2. "The Case of William Wieland," *Report of the Subcommittee to Investigate the Administration of the Internal Security Act and Other Internal Security Laws,* of the Com-

mittee on the Judiciary, State Department Security, 1962, pp. 1–3 and 92–130.

3. Aleksander Solzhenitsyn, "Misconceptions About Russia Are a Threat to America," *Foreign Affairs*, Spring, 1980, p. 826.

4. Austin J. App in Elizabeth Lutz, *German Women in Russian Hands*, (a pamphlet published in Philadelphia by Boniface Press, 1950), p. 46. See also, John Montgomery, *Hungary: The Unwilling Satellite*, New York, Devin-Adair, 1947, pp. 239–245. See also, John Noble, *I Was a Slave in Russia*, Devin-Adair, 1964, plus, a taped personal interview with a woman who was there. See also, George Racey Jordan, *From Major Jordan's Diaries*, Western Islands, 1962, p. 126 (deals with American financing of the Russian occupation forces in Eastern Europe).

5. R. J. Rummel, *Death by Government*, Transaction Publishers, New Brunswick, 1989, p. 8, lists 37,828,000 Chinese murdered by Chairman Mao. In an interview with Radio Liberty, Harry Wu suggests 80 million were murdered.

6. "An Examination of U.S. Policy Toward POW/MIAs," U.S. Senate Committee on Foreign Relations, May 23, 1991, pp. 3–22.

7. Nikolai Tolstoy, *The Secret Betrayal*, Charles Scribner's Sons, New York, 1977, p. 409. See also, Peter J. Huxley-Blythe, *The East Came West*, The Caxton Printers, Ltd., Caldwell, Idaho, 1964, p. 169. See also, Michael A. Ledeen, "It Didn't Start With Elian," *Wall Street Journal*, May 11, 2000, editorial page.

8. Ernest W. Lefever, *TV and National Defense*, Institute for American Strategy Press, Boston, Virginia, 22713.

9. John A. Stormer, *None Dare Call It Treason*, Liberty Bell Press, P. O. Box 32, Florissant, Missouri, 1964, pp. 8–14.

10. René A. Wormser, *Foundations: Their Power and Influence*, Devin-Adair Company, New York, 1958, pp. 174–186 and 331–333. Republished by Radio Liberty through Covenant House Books, Sevierville, Tennessee, 1993.

11. Dan Smoot, *The Invisible Government*, The Dan Smoot Report, 1962, republished by Western Islands in 1965.

12. Phyllis Schlafly, *A Choice Not An Echo*, Pere Marquette Press, P.O. Box 316, Alton, Illinois, pp. 102–116.

13. Carroll Quigley, *Tragedy and Hope: A History of the World in Our Time*, The Macmillan Company, New York, 1966, p. 950.

14. Ibid., p. 130.

15. (Cecil) Rhodes' *Confession of Faith*, op cit.

16. Quigley, op cit., p. 131.

17. Ibid., p. 137.

18. Ibid., See also, Thomas Pakenham, *The Boer War*, Random House, 1979, p. 120. Here Milner admits he intentionally precipitated the Boer War.

19. Pakenham, op cit, p. 607.

20. Quigley, op cit., p. 138.

21. Ibid., pp. 950–951.

22. See the video, *What Is Little Known About the History of Modern Wars*, available from Radio Liberty. According to Bertrand Russell in volume one of his autobiography, Edward Grey openly discussed his plan to create World War I. Grey signed secret agreements with both France and Russia that ensured the war. An extensive analysis of the origin of World War I, and of Sir Edward Grey's association with the Round Table is available in an unfinished manuscript from Radio Liberty.

23. Frederic C. Howe, *The Confessions of a Reformer*, Charles Scribner's Sons, 1925, pp. 295–305. See also, Quigley, op cit., p. 951.

24. Ibid., pp. 951–952.

25. Ibid., p. 866.

26. Ibid., pp. 1247–1248.

27. Ibid., p. 1201.

28. Ibid., pp. 618–639.

29. Ibid.

30. Ibid., p. 945.

31. Ibid.

32. Ibid., p. 956.

33. Ibid., pp. 937–948.

34. Professor Quigley discussed the suppression of his book in an audio-tape interview available from Radio Liberty.

35. Gary Allen and Larry Abraham, *None Dare Call It Conspiracy*, Concord Press, Rossmoor California, 1972, p. 107.

36. Antony C. Sutton, *Wall Street and the Rise of Hitler*, '76 Press, 1976.

37. Letter from William E. Dodd to Colonel House, October 29, 1936, Sterling Library, Yale University, New Haven, Connecticut.

38. Antony C. Sutton, *Western Technology and Soviet Economic Development, 1930 to 1945*, three-volume set, Hoover Institution Press, Stanford University, Stanford, Calif., Available from Radio Liberty.

39. Herbert Hoover, *The Memoirs of Herbert Hoover*, The Macmillan Company, New York, 1952, p. 420.

40. Antony C. Sutton, *National Suicide: Military Aid to the Soviet Union*, Arlington House, New Rochelle New York, 1974, p. 44.

41. See the videos *What Is Little Known About the History of Modern Wars*, and *The Best Enemies Money Can Buy*, available from Radio Liberty.

Chapter Four

the Final secret

One wintry afternoon in February 1891, three men were engaged in earnest conversation in London. From that conversation were to flow consequences of the greatest importance to the British Empire and to the world as a whole. For these men were organizing a secret society that was, for more than fifty years, to be one of the most important forces in the formulation and execution of British imperial and foreign policy.[1]

At this point we must return to Agatha Christie's story. When Monsieur Poirot completed questioning the passengers on the Orient Express, he was amazed to find that all of them had either known Daisy Armstrong, or a member of her family, and all of them had a motive to kill Mr. Ratchet, a.k.a. Crosetti. The inspector also suspected they were all concealing what they knew about the crime. He wondered how he would solve the murder when there were so many suspects and so many clues. We face the same problem today. Many groups and organizations are working to establish a world government and a new world religion. The media is lying to us, conservative organizations are deceiving us, and our political leaders are doing everything possible to keep us from learning the identity of our enemy.

Professor Carroll Quigley died in 1976, and to my knowledge no one had tried to validate his research. In 1980, I decided to find out how he knew about Cecil Rhodes' secret society since there were no references or footnotes in his book. I contacted the History Department at Georgetown University where Professor Quigley taught, and I was told that his papers had been donated to their library. I closed my medical practice, traveled to Washington, D.C., and began reading through thousands of pages of notes, correspondence, and unfinished manuscripts. I found what I was looking for among his letters. Professor Quigley went to England shortly after World War II ended, and while there he met Sir Alfred Zimmern. Sir Alfred taught International Relations at Oxford University, and since both men were historians and shared similar interests, they soon became friends. Eventually Sir Alfred told Professor Quigley about Cecil Rhodes' secret society. The members of the organization called it "the Group," or "the Band," or simply "Us."[2] Sir Alfred joined the movement in 1910 and remained within the inner circle of the Group until 1922 when he stopped attending meetings because he disagreed with their plan to support Germany. He was also concerned because they supported Adolph Hitler during the years that led up to World War II.[3]

Sir Alfred asked Professor Quigley not to reveal his source of information, although he had no objection to him writing about the secret society. Based on what he learned from Sir Alfred, and ten years of his own research, Professor Quigley eventually wrote a book entitled *The Anglo-American Estab-*

lishment, but he couldn't get it published. Why? Because even back in the 1950s most of our publishing houses were controlled by the Eastern Establishment. In those days there were only a few conservative publishers, and since Professor Quigley detested conservatives, he didn't contact them.[4] His manuscript languished among his papers until four years after his death when an obscure publisher got permission to print it.[5] The information I learned from studying Professor Quigley's papers and reading his second book, *The Anglo-American Establishment*, helped me understand part of the story of Cecil Rhodes' secret society, but there was much more.

Professor Quigley wrote:

> **I have been told that the story I relate here would be better left untold, since it would provide ammunition for the enemies of what I admire. I do not share this view. The last thing I should wish is that anything I write could be used by the Anglophobes and isolationists of the *Chicago Tribune*. But I feel that the truth has a right to be told, and, once told, can be an injury to no men of good will.[6]**

Professor Quigley was right. The truth must be told, and we are indebted to him for his years of diligent research. He continued:

> **. . . it would have been very difficult to write this book if I had not received a certain amount of assistance of a personal nature from persons close to the Group. For obvious reasons, I cannot reveal the names of such persons. . . .[7]**

Later he wrote:

> **Sir Alfred Zimmern, for example, while always close to the Group, was in its inner circle only for a brief period in**

1910–1922, thereafter slowly drifting away into the outer orbits of the Group.[8]

Professor Quigley described the formation of Cecil Rhodes' secret society:

> **One wintry afternoon in February 1891, three men were engaged in earnest conversation in London. From that conversation were to flow consequences of the greatest importance to the British Empire and to the world as a whole. For these men were organizing a secret society that was, for more than fifty years, to be one of the most important forces in the formulation and execution of British imperial and foreign policy. . . .** [9]
>
> **The Rhodes Scholarships, established by the terms of Cecil Rhodes's seventh will, are known to everyone. What is not so widely known is that Rhodes in five previous wills left his fortune to form a secret society, which was to devote itself to the preservation and expansion of the British Empire. And what does not seem to be known to anyone is that this secret society was created by Rhodes and his principal trustee, Lord Milner, and continues to exist to this day.** [10]

Sir Alfred was not Professor Quigley's only source of information. There were many others; I have listed four of them below as 1, 2, 3, and 4. I discovered three additional sources which are listed as 5, 6, and 7.

1) William T. Stead was a member of Cecil Rhodes' secret society, but he was expelled because he opposed the Boer War. Some years later he wrote about the society in *The Last Will and Testament of Cecil John Rhodes*, in an article in *Review of Reviews*, and in his diary. Frederic Whyte wrote a bi-

ography of William T. Stead based on his diary. The following quotation is taken from that biography. There we learn that Rhodes visited Stead in February 1891, and:

> **The talk concentrated presently upon the Secret Society— the Society of the Elect [Rhodes liked that word] who were to bind themselves to work for the British Empire in the way in which the Jesuits worked for the Church of Rome. . . . I telegraphed for Brett, who came two hours later and we had a long talk. The net upshot of which was that the ideal arrangement would be, so far as we could see at present: Rhodes, General of the Society; Stead, Brett, Milner, to be the Junta of three. After Rhodes, Stead to be General, with a third, who might be Rothschild in succession; behind them, Manning, the Booths, little Johnston, Albert Grey, Arthur Balfour, to constitute a circle of Initiates.[11]**

The fact that Arthur Balfour was chosen to become a member of the Circle of Initiates is important. You will learn more about him as our story progresses. Eleven years later, in 1902, Arthur Balfour became the prime minister of Great Britain.

2) Professor Quigley discovered a copy of Cecil Rhodes' *Confession of Faith* among Lord Milner's papers. There Cecil Rhodes asked the rhetorical question:

> **Why should we not form a secret society with but one object, the furtherance of the British Empire, for the bringing of the whole uncivilized world under British rule for the recovery of the United States, for the making the Anglo-Saxon race but one Empire.**

Rhodes' *Confession of Faith* was attached to the first five of his seven wills. It was not included in his last two wills because the secret society was formed in February 1891.[12]

3) Professor Quigley was allowed to examine the Round Table Group's secret records.[13]

4) Extensive documentation of the fact that Cecil Rhodes created a secret society can be found in chapter three of Professor Quigley's book, *The Anglo-American Establishment*.[14]

5) H. G. Wells wrote about the secret society in his book, *The New Machiavelli*. In an earlier book, *Experiment in Autobiography*, he wrote about a dinner club he had belonged to called the Coefficients. The members were recruited from two groups. Bertrand Russell, George Bernard Shaw, H. G. Wells, and Sidney Webb represented the Fabian Socialists; Lord Milner, Leopold Amery, Lord Brand, Sir Edward Grey, Lord Cecil, and several others represented the British aristocracy.[15] Lord Milner, Lord Brand, and Leo Amery were also members of Rhodes' secret society, and Sir Edward Grey was either a member, or closely aligned with it.[16] The two groups controlled the foreign and domestic policy of Great Britain for many years. Leo Amery joined Rhodes' secret society during the Boer War, and remained a member during the remainder of his life. In 1940, he rose from his seat in Parliament, pointed at Prime Minister Neville Chamberlain, and shouted:

> **You have sat too long here for any good you have been doing. Depart, I say—let us have done with you. In the name of God, go!**[17]

Neville Chamberlain resigned several days later, and Winston Churchill became the prime minister of Great Britain. Was he a member of the secret society? I don't know, but I have a copy of a letter he sent to H. G. Wells in which wrote:

> It is quite impossible, as I am sure you realize, for me to
> discuss these matters outside the secret circle. . . .[18]

In chapter one, I noted Winston Churchill's reference to Lord Tennyson's poem, "Locksley Hall," as "the most wonderful of modern prophesies." Why did Churchill support Cecil Rhodes' effort to federate the world? The answer to that question will surprise you.

Although H. G. Wells' book *The New Machiavelli* was a work of fiction, he described the Coefficients but renamed the dinner club The Pentagram Circle. That was an odd name for a group of the most prominent men in Great Britain, but as our story progresses you will understand why he used that name. He called Rhodes' secret society The Confederates. It was led by a German named Crupp, a pseudonym for Lord Milner, who was German. The following conversation can be found on page 340 of *The New Machiavelli*. The character who represented H. G. Wells asked Crupp (Lord Milner):

> "Are you a Confederate?" I asked suddenly.
>
> "That's a secret nobody tells," he said.
>
> "What are the Confederates after?"
>
> "Making aristocracy work, I suppose. Just as, I gather, you want to do."
>
> The Confederates were being heard of at that time. They were at once attractive and repellent to me, an odd secret society whose membership nobody knew, pledged, it was said, to impose . . . an ample constructive policy upon the Conservatives. In the press, at any rate, they had an air of deliberately organized power. . . .[19]

6) Frederic Howe was never aware of Rhodes' secret society, but Lord Milner's men told him about their plan to unite the

world when he met them at the Paris Peace Conference in
1919. Since he was a well-known peace activist, President
Wilson asked him to review the English and French treaties
related to the disposition of Palestine after the war. Frederic
Howe believed in the sanctity of treaties; he was convinced
that Great Britain was forced to enter the war because of a
fifty-year-old treaty with Belgium. He justified the carnage
that followed because he was convinced that nations must
honor their treaties if there was ever to be world peace
through world law. He wrote:

> The secret treaties were placed at my disposal by Colonel
> House and the English authorities. . . . They furnished as-
> tounding revelations. Our allies, like Germany, scrapped
> treaties—not with traditional enemies, but solemn agree-
> ments with friends and with each other. The documents
> showed that England and France had pleaded with the King
> of the Hedjas to throw the Arab forces in with the allied
> cause, and drive the Turks from Arabia. The Arabs were
> promised their freedom in exchange; . . . Scarcely was the
> ink dry on their compact with the Arabs when they negoti-
> ated with each other the secret Sykes-Picot Treaty, under
> whose terms England was to retain Mesopotamia, France
> was to keep Syria. . . . Then the Jews asked for Palestine,
> and Balfour, the gentleman-statesman, agreed on behalf
> of England that they should have it, although Palestine
> had already been promised to the Arabs and given to the
> French.[20]

When Frederic Howe realized that neither England nor
France honored their treaties, he was devastated. He surmised
there must have been another reason Great Britain entered
the war. Some observers said the war was fought for "economic imperialism," and that Britain entered the war to ex-

pand her commercial empire. When Frederic Howe met Lord Milner's men, he learned the real reason for the conflict. In his book, *The Confessions of a Reformer,* he wrote:

> **One evening a number of young Englishmen visited me at the Hotel Chatham. They were Oxford and Cambridge men, brilliant, friendly, amiable. A few days later I was invited to breakfast with them. Arriving, I found that I was at the house of Lloyd George; that Philip Kerr, my host, was Lloyd George's secretary. He and his associates, Lionel Curtis, Arnold Toynbee, and others, were known as "Lord Milner's men." They were editors of the periodical known as The Round Table, and had organized an imperial conference in each of the British colonies. . . . It astounded me to find that they scarcely knew the meaning of the words "economic imperialism." Imperialism was not economic, it was a white man's burden. A sacred trust, undertaken for the well-being of peoples unfitted for self-government. The war was in no way related to the conflict of financial interests. . . . This imperialism, which was not imperialism, must be carried to the end. It must be carried by Anglo-Saxons, and England was no longer able to carry it alone. She had lost much of her best blood in the trenches; Oxford and Cambridge . . . had been depleted of a generation of talent. The only country which could be trusted to share the white man's burden was America; America must help. She must carry it. . . .[21]**

Why was World War I fought? Because of "imperialism that was not imperialism," because of the

> **. . . white man's burden. A sacred trust undertaken to provide for the well-being of peoples unfitted for self-government.**

World War I was fought to bring all nations under the control
of a world authority. When the conflict finally ended, Great
Britain was bankrupt, and Lord Milner's men asked Frederic Howe to arrange a meeting with the American delegation
to determine if they were willing to assume the leadership of
their program. Colonel House led the American delegation,
and he and his associates readily agreed to the British offer.[22]
Subsequently, Royal Institutes of International Affairs were
established in five Commonwealth nations, and the Council
on Foreign Relations was organized in the United States.[23]
When it became obvious that the League of Nations was destined to fail, the newly formed Anglo-American Establishment
began financing the Nazis, which led to World War II.[24]

7) Following World War I, Colonel House and J. P. Morgan created the Council on Foreign Relations as a front for
the American branch of the Round Table, and Morgan's financial empire.[25] Admiral Chester Ward belonged to the CFR
for sixteen years, and in his book, *Kissinger on the Couch*, he
warned that the small group that controlled the organization
sought

> ... disarmament and submergence of U.S. sovereignty and
> national independence into an all-powerful one-world gov-
> ernment. ...

He continued:

> [The] CFR as such does not write the platforms of both
> political parties or select their respective presidential can-
> didates. . . . But CFR members, as individuals, acting in
> concert with other individual CFR members, do.
>
> Thus, David Rockefeller does not exercise ... vast pow-
> ers because he is chairman of the board of directors of CFR,

but because he is chairman of the board of one of the two most powerful banks in the world . . . his influence extends into finance, business, industry, transportation, communications, the press, television, universities, foundations, international organizations, and government. He has similar influence throughout the Free World, and is now rapidly expanding into the Communist world.[26]

When Inspector Poirot finished questioning the passengers on the Orient Express, he was left with two possible explanations for the crime. The evidence suggested that someone had boarded the train, killed Crosetti, and escaped, but the Inspector knew most of the evidence was contrived. The second possibility was that all of the passengers were involved. Since there were twelve passengers, and twelve stab wounds in the victim's body, each of them must have stabbed him once. Inspector Poirot assembled everyone in the lounge car and announced that he had solved the crime. First, he discussed the possibility that an unknown person killed Crosetti, but he promptly ruled out that theory. Then he noted that each of the passengers had both a motive and an opportunity to commit the crime, and suggested that all of them were involved. When he finished his presentation, several of the passengers began to weep, while others sat stoically, realizing their plot had been discovered.

They had all participated in the murder because Crosetti had escaped punishment. Suddenly Inspector Poirot changed his line of reasoning and announced that he planned to tell the police that the killer must have escaped since it was ridiculous to suggest they were all guilty. As the movie ended the passengers breathed a collective sigh of relief and began to celebrate their success. What does Agatha Christie's story have to do with The Brotherhood of Darkness? It has everything to do with it. All of the groups listed in chapter two are working to establish a new world order and a new world religion, with the exception of the Jews as a race. Our enemy is not a race or a religion. It is a spiritual movement that involves people of all races and all religions . . . including some apostate Jews. How can we understand what is happening today? I am about to reveal a secret that has eluded most researchers and most historians.

Professor Quigley told us that Cecil John Rhodes created a secret society to bring the uncivilized world under the control of the British Empire and reunite the United States with England. Frank Aydelotte, the American director of the Rhodes Trust, added that Rhodes wanted to organize

. . . so great a power as to hereafter render wars impossible. . . .[27]

That concept gradually evolved into the current effort to unify the world. Professor Quigley believed Rhodes' idea originated with Professor John Ruskin who taught Art Appreciation at Oxford University during the early years of the second half of the nineteenth century. Professor Quigley told us that Cecil Rhodes attended Professor Ruskin's inaugural lecture in 1870, copied the lecture in long- hand, and carried it with him the rest of his life.[28] That is true, but the most important part of the story has been ignored. Professor Quigley failed to grasp the significance of the fact that John Ruskin was an occultist.[29] Through the centuries, some men and women have sought the forbidden knowledge, and if they discovered it they fulfilled their obligation by dedicating their lives to uniting the world. Plato advocated that goal, and John Ruskin read Plato every day.[30] When Cecil Rhodes heard Professor Ruskin's clarion call, he was consumed with a desire to dedicate his life to uniting the world. Others who fell under Ruskin's influence joined him, but most of them were under the influence of another power, the second most important power in the world.[31]

Earlier I quoted part of Cecil Rhodes' *Confession of Faith*, but I left out the most important part. He wrote:

> **In the present day I become a member of the Masonic order. I see the wealth and power they possess, the influence they hold, and I think over their ceremonies and I wonder that a large body of men can devote themselves to what at times appears the most ridiculous and absurd rites without an object and without an end. The idea gleaming and dancing before one's eyes like a will-o-the-wisp at last frames itself into a plan. Why should we not form a secret society with but one object, the furtherance of the British Empire, for the bringing of the whole uncivilized world under British rule for the recovery of the United States, for the making the Anglo-Saxon race but one Empire.[32]**

Although Cecil Rhodes never understood the Masonic rites, or the significance of the oaths he took, he remained in the Lodge because it gave him access to the money he needed to purchase the gold and diamond mines of southern Africa. If you study the lives of those who joined him, you will discover that most of them were either Freemasons, spiritualists, Theosophists, or members of the Society for Psychical Research. Lord Milner was a 33rd Degree Mason, William T. Stead was a spiritualist and a Theosophist, and Arthur Balfour was a spiritualist, a Mason, and a member of the Society for Psychical Research. What most researchers have missed is the fact that most of the men who joined Cecil Rhodes' secret society were involved in the occult.[33]

Professor Quigley discussed the two power blocs that controlled Great Britain during the early decades of the twentieth century. One was led by Lord Cecil, the other by Lord Milner. Professor Quigley wrote:

> **One of the enduring creations of the Cecil Bloc is the Society for Psychical Research, which holds a position in the history of the Cecil Bloc similar to that held by the Royal Institute of International Affairs in the Milner Group. The Society was founded in 1882 by the Balfour family and their in-laws. . . . In the twentieth century it was dominated by those members of the Cecil Bloc who became most readily members of the Milner Group.**[34]

Thus we learn that most of those who joined the Milner Group were members of the Society for Psychical Research. According to the International Edition of the *Encyclopedia Americana*, the Society was organized to study occultism. Lord Tennyson's uncle, the Balfour family, and their in-laws, formed the Society for Psychical Research, and Alfred Lord Tennyson was a member.[35]

To grasp the significance of what is happening today, you must understand the oaths that Cecil Rhodes and many of his followers took when they became Masons. When a candidate is inducted into the First Degree of the Blue Lodge, he is blindfolded, a noose is place around his neck, his left chest is bared, his left pants leg is rolled up, and he is told to take off his shoes and kneel before the Worshipful Master of his Lodge.[36] He must then swear that he will never reveal what he is about to learn. Although there are some minor variations in wording throughout the world, all Masonic oaths are similar in content. Upon entering the Entered Apprentice degree, each candidate must swear:

All this I most solemnly, sincerely promise and swear, with a firm and steadfast resolution to perform the same, without any mental reservation or secret evasion of mind whatever, binding myself under no less penalty than that of having my throat cut across, my tongue torn out by it roots, and my body buried in the rough sands of the sea, at low-water mark, where the tide ebbs and flows twice in twenty-four hours, should I ever knowingly violate this, my Entered Apprentice obligation, so help me God. . . .[37]

When a candidate enters the Fellow Craft, or second degree of Masonry, he agrees to have the following done to him if he ever violates his oaths of secrecy:

. . . my breast torn open, my heart plucked out, and given as prey to the birds of the air and the beasts of the field. . . .[38]

Upon entering the third degree, the Initiate agrees to have his

. . . body severed in twain, my bowels taken from thence and burned to ashes, and scattered before the four winds of heaven. . . .[39]

During each ceremony the candidate is asked, "What do you desire most?" He is told to respond either "the Light" or "more Light," but he is never told what the Light represents. Christians who have prayed the Sinners Prayer know that when they invited Jesus into their heart, something happened, and their lives were transformed. In a similar manner, when an initiate kneels before his Worshipful Master and asks for the Light, something happens, and his world view changes. Unless he renounces his oaths, and leaves the Lodge, he will never again be the same. What happens when an initiate asks the Light into his life? I am about to reveal the secret the Elect have guarded for thousands of years. Let me warn you that once you learn it, you will never again look at things in the same way again.

Albert Pike was the leading Masonic philosopher of the nineteenth century, and he remains the most revered Mason of all time. His body is interred at the House of the Temple in Washington, D.C., and his statue stands close by. Until 1974 his book, *Morals and Dogma*, was given to every Scottish Rite Freemason who reached the 14th Degree, and it is still recommended on all Masonic reading lists.[40] On page 104 of *Morals and Dogma*, Albert Pike referred to "the Truth which it calls 'Light.'" He wrote:

> **Masonry . . . conceals its secrets from all except the Adepts and Sages, or the Elect, and uses false explanations and misinterpretations of its symbols to mislead those who deserve only to be misled; to conceal the Truth, which it calls Light, from them, and to draw them away from it.**[41]

That is an incredible statement. Albert Pike admits there is an intentional effort to deceive Initiates who enter the Lodge about

> **. . . the Truth, which it calls Light.**

On page 819 of *Morals and Dogma*, Albert Pike reveals that:

> **The Blue Degrees are but the outer court or portico of the Temple. Part of the symbols are displayed there to the Initiate, but he is intentionally misled by false interpretations. It is not intended that he shall understand them; but it is**

**intended that he shall imagine he understands them. Their
true explication is reserved for the Adepts, the Princes of
Masonry.**

The Blue Degrees are the first three levels of Masonry. Once
again, Albert Pike admits that there is an intentional effort to
deceive those who enter the Craft. Why are they misled? Because if Initiates understood the true implications of the
Masonic ceremonies, most of them would flee in terror. On
page 781 of *Morals and Dogma* we read:

**If you reflect, my Brother . . . you will no doubt suspect
that some secret meaning was concealed in these words.**

What was concealed? Albert Pike tells us that the Rites of
Masonry are used to conceal ". . . some secret meaning . . . "
but he never tells his readers what the "secret meaning" represents. On page 219 we read:

**That Rite raises a corner of the veil, even in the Degree of
Apprentice; for it there declares that Masonry is a worship.**

Albert Pike tells us that "Masonry is a worship," yet Masons
deny the Craft is a religion. How can there be worship without a religion? Who do they worship? They worship the Great
Architect of the Universe, but most Masons have no idea what
that entity represents. On page 840 of *Morals and Dogma* we
learn:

**It was the remembrance of this scientific and religious
Absolute, of this doctrine that is summed up in a word, of
this Word, in fine, alternately lost and found again, that
was transmitted to the Elect of all the Ancient Initiations:**

> it was this same remembrance, preserved, or perhaps pro-
> faned in the celebrated Order of the Templars, that became
> for all the secret associations, of the Rose-Croix, of the Il-
> luminati, and of the Hermetic Freemasons, the reason of
> their strange rites, of their signs more or less convention-
> al, and, above all, of their mutual devotedness and of their
> power.

That statement was designed to help those entering the 32nd Degree of the Scottish Rite understand the secret of Masonry. They are told that the ". . . Word . . ." (the secret knowledge) was transmitted to the leaders of the Ancient Initiations (the Elect), preserved by the Templars, and then passed down through the Rose-Croix (the Rosicrucians), and the Illuminati to the Hermetic Freemasons (the Masons). The "Word," or secret knowledge was incorporated into the symbolism of their rites. What is the "secret"? When an initiate learns the mystery of his Craft he has access to "power."

Manly P. Hall was the leading Masonic philosopher of the twentieth century. His book, *Lectures on Ancient Philosophy*, reveals there are two levels of Masonry, an outer fraternity everyone knows about, and an inner fraternity dedicated to the study of "the mysterious *arcanum arcanorum*." Manly P. Hall wrote:

> Freemasonry is a fraternity within a fraternity—an outer
> organization concealing an inner brotherhood of the elect.
> . . . The visible society is a splendid camaraderie of "free
> and accepted" men enjoined to devote themselves to ethi-
> cal, educational, fraternal, patriotic, and humanitarian
> concerns. The invisible society is a secret and most august
> fraternity whose members are dedicated to the service of a
> mysterious *arcanum arcanorum*.[42]

You cannot understand the significance of either the dark force that energized Cecil John Rhodes, or the strange symbol on the back of the dollar bill, until you understand the mysterious *"arcanum arcanorum."* Have you ever wondered why there is an unfinished pyramid capped by an "all-seeing eye" on our currency? Experts tell us:

> **The Eye of God on the seal is a symbol representing spiritual vision that was used in many secret societies, including the Rosicrucians and the Freemasons. The pyramid is a symbol of material power and was used by many ancient cultures as an initiation chamber.**[43]

The number thirteen denotes evil and bad luck. Superstition holds that Friday the thirteenth is a dangerous date, and many hotels don't have a thirteenth floor, but few people know why. Jacques De Molay, the leader of the Knights Templars, was arrested on Friday, October 13, 1307.[44] Other writers tell us:

> **. . . the number thirteen embodies a key quality for the United States, as it appears repeatedly in the Great Seal as well as being the number of original colonies. Throughout the seal the number thirteen is used thirteen times—in the number of stars, clouds around the stars, stripes, arrows, leaves and berries in the olive branches, feathers in the tail, layers of stones in the pyramid, number of letters in *E Pluribus Unum* and in *Annuit Coeptus*. . . .**[45]

The term *Novus Ordo Seclorum* beneath the pyramid alludes to the "New Secular Order" that is coming. The Roman numeral MDCCLXXVI (1776) refers to the year our Declaration of Independence was signed, as well as the year the Illuminati was created.

Manly P. Hall explained the origin of the occult emblem on the back of the dollar bill.

> **For more than three thousand years, secret societies have labored to create the background of knowledge necessary to the establishment of an enlightened democracy among the nations of the world. . . .[46]**

> **Men bound by a secret oath to labor in the cause of world democracy decided that in the American colonies they would plant the roots of a new way of life. Brotherhoods were established to meet secretly, and they quietly and industriously conditioned America to its destiny for leadership in a free world. . . .[47]**

> **On the reverse of our nation's Great Seal is an unfinished pyramid to represent human society itself, imperfect and incomplete. Above floats the symbol of the esoteric orders, the radiant triangle with its all-seeing eye. . . . There is only one possible origin for these symbols, and that is the secret societies which came to this country 150 years before the Revolutionary War.[48]**

The emblem was placed on the back of the Great Seal of the United States in 1789, and hidden from public view until Henry Wallace convinced President Roosevelt it should be displayed on the back of the dollar bill. Both Henry Wallace and President Roosevelt were 32nd Degree Masons. Henry Wallace was also involved in other occult activities.[49]

Some historians trace the origin of modern-day Masonry back to the Knights Templar, a religious order that was organized in Jerusalem in 1118. The Templars were supposed to guard the pilgrims traveling to the Holy Land, but many of

them were far more interested in learning the forbidden
knowledge of the Sages. After the Moslems seized Jerusalem
in 1187, a group of Templars returned to Europe and used
their esoteric knowledge to amass a great deal of wealth. They
soon became the central bankers of Europe, and both the
Catholic Church and the monarchies began borrowing from
them. It seemed that everything the Templars did turned a
healthy profit. Then, in 1307, Jacques de Molay, their leader,
was arrested and accused of heresy; several years later he
was burned at the stake.[50] Some of his followers escaped to
Scotland, where they lived out their lives in obscurity. Many
people believe that modern-day Masonry carries on the traditions of the Templars because both the York Rite and the
Scottish Rites of Freemasonry offer Knights Templar degrees.[51]

Catholic historians claim the Order was suppressed because it blasphemed God, and note that many Templars con-
fessed their heresy. Masonic researchers claim the Templars
were outlawed because the papacy and the monarchies didn't
want to repay their loans, and the confessions were invalid
because they were extracted by torture.[52] How can we discover the truth about the suppression of the Knights Templars? Manly P. Hall had access to the hidden knowledge. He
wrote:

> **Was Jacques de Molay burned by the Holy Inquisition
> merely because he wore the red cross of the Templar? What
> were those secrets to which he was true even in death? Did
> his companion knights perish with him merely because they
> had amassed a fortune and exercised an unusual degree of
> temporal power? . . . It was not the physical power of the
> Templars, but the knowledge which they had brought with
> them from the East, that the church feared. The Templars**

had discovered part of the great *arcanum;* they had become wise in those mysteries which had been celebrated
in Mecca thousands of years before the advent of Moham-
med: they had read a few pages from the dread book of the
Anthropos, and for this knowledge they were doomed to
die.[53]

According to Manly P. Hall, the Templars were suppressed
because they discovered the secret of "the dread book of the
Anthropos." Now you must reread the instructions given to
candidates entering the 32nd Degree of Masonry:

> It was the remembrance of this scientific and religious
> Absolute, of this doctrine that is summed up in a word, of
> this Word, in fine, alternately lost and found again, that
> was transmitted to the Elect of all the Ancient Initiations:
> it was this same remembrance, preserved, or perhaps pro-
> faned in the celebrated Order of the Templars, that became
> for all the secret associations, of the Rose-Croix, of the Il-
> luminati, and of the Hermetic Freemasons, the reason of
> their strange rites, of their signs more or less convention-
> al, and, above all, of their mutual devotedness and of their
> power.[54]

Albert Pike goes on to explain that the secret of Masonry originated with the Ancient Magi, was imperfectly revealed by
the Gnostics, and guessed at by the Templars. He writes:

> The Occult Science of the Ancient Magi was concealed
> under the shadows of the Ancient Mysteries: it was imper-
> fectly revealed or rather disfigured by the Gnostics; it is
> guessed at under the obscurities that cover the pretended
> crimes of the Templars; and it is found enveloped in enig-

mas that seem impenetrable, in the Rites of the Highest Masonry.

Magism was the Science of Abraham and Orpheus, of Confucius and Zoroaster. It was the dogmas of this Science that were engraven on the tables of stone by Hanoch and Trismegistus.[55]

Here we learn that the secret of Masonry can be found in the teachings of Zoroaster. His followers believe there are two gods, a good god and an evil god, a God of Light and a God of Darkness; the evil god is also known as "the Demon." They believe the two forces are in constant conflict, and according to Albert Pike, the battle began in the Garden of Eden. He tells us:

> ... the Prince of Darkness ... made Adam, whose soul was of the Divine Light, contributed by the Eons, and his body of matter, so that he belonged to both Empires, that of Light and that of Darkness. To prevent the light from escaping at once, the Demons forbade Adam to eat the fruit of "knowledge of good and evil," by which he would have known the Empire of Light and that of Darkness. He obeyed; an Angel of Light induced him to transgress, and gave him the means of victory; but the Demons created Eve, who seduced him. . . .[56]

This is one of the most important passages you will ever encounter. Reread it several times. According to Albert Pike, our Lord was "the Prince of Darkness," and "the Demon." The Serpent of Eden, was "an Angel of Light." Is this madness, or something far more sinister?

What is the secret that has been handed down through the ages? The answer can be found on page 321 of *Morals and Dogma*, where you will discover the source of "the Light" that Masons seek. Albert Pike wrote:

> ... Lucifer, the Light-bearer! Strange and mysterious name to give to the Spirit of Darkness! Lucifer, the Son of the Morning! Is it he who bears the Light, and with its splendors intolerable blinds feeble, sensual, or selfish Souls? Doubt it not! for traditions are full of Divine Revelations and Inspirations. . . .[57]

Manly P. Hall clarified Albert Pike's statement when he wrote:

> When the Mason learns that the key to the warrior on the block is the proper application of the dynamo of living power, he has learned the mystery of his Craft. The seething energies of Lucifer are in his hands. . . .[58]

Helena Petrovna Blavatsky became a Mason, and later channeled the three volumes of her book *The Secret Doctrine*. Adolph Hitler, Margaret Sanger, Thomas Edison, William T. Stead, Arthur Conan Doyle, Henry Wallace, and many others read her books and embraced her philosophy.[59] Her beliefs are the basis of Alice Bailey's writings, the Lucis Trust, and the New Age movement. In volume two of *The Secret Doctrine*, Madame Helena Petrovna Blavatsky wrote:

> In this case it is but natural . . . to view Satan, the Serpent of Genesis, as the real creator and benefactor, the Father of Spiritual mankind. For it is he who was the "Harbinger of Light," bright radiant Lucifer, who opened the eyes of the automaton created by Jehovah, as alleged; and he who was the first to whisper: "in the day ye eat thereof ye shall be as Elohim, knowing good and evil"—can only be regarded in the light of a Saviour. . . .[60]

And now it stands proven that Satan, or the Red Fiery Dragon, the "Lord of Phosphorus" (brimstone was a theological improvement), and Lucifer, or "Light Bearer," is in us: it is our Mind—our tempter and Redeemer, our intelligent liberator and Saviour from pure animalism. Without this principle . . . we would be surely no better than animals.[61]

Now you know the secret that has been passed down through the ages. The Ancient Magi, the Adepts of the Mystery Religions, the followers of Confucius and Zoroaster, the Templars, the Rosicrucians, the Illuminati, and the Hermetic Freemasons all worshiped Lucifer. In return, he gave them wealth and power. Most Masons have no understanding of the mysterious *arcanum arcanorum*, but they are used by those who do. The occult religions are only part of our problem. The Council on Foreign Relations, the Bilderbergers, the Trilateral Commission, the Club of Rome, and almost all of the other groups listed in chapter two can be traced back to the occult.

Six of our last nine presidents have been members of the Council on Foreign Relations, and at least five of our last eleven presidents have been Masons.[62] Another president, William Jefferson Clinton, was a senior member of the de Molays, a boys' club for Masons, which explains why the Republican senators who are Masons opposed his impeachment. President Roosevelt and President Truman packed the United States Supreme Court with Masons, and between 1941 and 1971 they controlled the highest court in our land. During that thirty-year period, they removed God, prayer, and the Bible from our schools in an effort to destroy the Christian heritage of our nation. They also centralized power in Washington, D.C., in an effort to destroy our federal system.[63]

The leaders of Masonry are working to replace our republican form of government with an authoritarian system, create a nonsectarian religion, and unite the world under their control. Their plan was laid out in the *New Age* magazine in 1950:

> **God's plan is dedicated to the unification of all races, religions and creeds. This plan, dedicated to the new order of things, is to make all things new—a new nation, a new race, a new civilization and a new religion, a nonsectarian religion that has already been recognized and called the religion of "The Great Light."**
>
> **Looking back into history, we can easily see that the Guiding Hand of Providence has chosen the Nordic people to bring in and unfold the new order of the world. . . . Providence has chosen the Nordics because the Nordics have prepared themselves and have chosen God. . . .**[64]

Now you know the secret of the Ages, and I can answer the questions that were raised in previous chapters.

Benjamin Disraeli wrote *Coningsby*. In that novel, a financier named Sidonia claimed the world was ruled by a secret cabal. Disraeli was obviously referring to Nathan Rothschild, who was the most powerful financier in the world at that time, and since Nathan Rothschild was Jewish, Disraeli's book has been used to document the existence of a Jewish conspiracy. Why did Benjamin Disraeli promote that belief when both he and Nathan Rothschild were Jewish? I believe it was because both men were Masons. The Lodge has always sought to divert attention away from its influence, and anti-Semitism has been used to conceal Satan's agenda. Both the America Civil Liberties Union and the Anti-Defamation League have strong ties to Masonry, which explains their anti-Christian bias, and why the ADL criticized Senator Lieberman, a practicing Jew, when he advocated religion-based morality during the 2000 elections.[65]

J. P. Morgan was instrumental in forcing our country into World War I. He and his associates funded the Bolsheviks and the Nazis, and he helped organize the Council on Foreign Relations. Occult writers tell us he based his investment strategy on astrology.[66]

Henry Ford built automotive factories for both the communists and the Nazis, received a medal from Adolph Hitler, and wrote *The International Jew*, which claimed that Jewish bankers financed Bolshevism. He distributed anti-Semitic material through his newspaper, and his closest friend, Thomas Edison, was a Theosophist.[67] The Ford Foundation has funded a number of communist front organizations, and was cited by a Senate investigating committee for financing the Institute of Pacific Relations which brought communism to China. Henry Ford was both a spiritualist and a 33rd Degree Mason. Why was he given Masonry's highest degree when he was known to be an anti-Semite?[68]

Andrew Carnegie and Cecil Rhodes were friends. The directors of the Carnegie Endowment for International Peace planned World War I, and then mounted a propaganda campaign to force us into that war. They financed the Lucis Trust and have worked to establish a world government. Andrew Carnegie was a spiritualist.[69]

Colonel Edward Mandell House manipulated the leaders of the Western world during the early decades of the twentieth century, and helped J. P. Morgan organize the Council on Foreign Relations after World War I. I found a copy of the *Protocols of the Learned Elders of Zion* among House's papers at Yale University, which suggests he was involved with either the writing or the distribution of that scurrilous document. New Age writers tell us he was an occultist.[70]

President Truman carried a copy of Lord Tennyson's poem in his wallet throughout his life. He packed the United States Supreme Court with Masons, ceded China and Eastern Europe to the communists, created the United Nations, involved us in a no-win war in Korea, and fired General MacArthur when he wanted to win that war. Harry Truman was a 33rd Degree Mason.[71]

Winston Churchill referred to Lord Tennyson's poem as, "the most wonderful of modern prophecies." During World War I he was responsible for the British invasion of Gallipoli where 216,000 British soldiers and 150,000 Turks fell in battle.[72] During World War II he insisted on the invasion of North Africa despite the opposition of our military planners. Then he did everything he could to delay the invasion of Europe; he opposed an invasion of southern France, insisted on invading Italy, brought Marshall Tito to power in Yugoslavia despite the fact he was a communist, and intentionally prolonged the war for over a year. That delay resulted in millions of additional deaths.[73] Most Holocaust victims were killed during the closing months of the war; had the Allies been allowed to invade Europe in 1943, most of the Jews would have been spared.[74] Winston Churchill was both a Mason and a Druid. He wanted to demonstrate the futility of war, and he succeeded.[75]

How can we understand such crass indifference to human suffering? Remember Manly P. Hall's words:

When the Mason learns that the key to the warrior on the block is the proper application of the dynamo of living power, he has learned the mystery of his Craft. The seething energies of Lucifer are in his hands. . . .[76]

Does the average Mason understand what is happening? Of

course not, but most of them believe our country should be a secular society, and they work toward that goal. Unfortunately the oaths they have taken cloud their understanding of the spiritual battle in which we are engaged.

What part does communism play? Rev. Richard Wurmbrand was living in Romania when the communists took over that country. He was arrested, imprisoned, and tortured for fourteen years to force him to renounce his faith. Many of the ministers who were imprisoned with him recanted their beliefs under torture, and they died broken men. When Rev. Wurmbrand was finally released, he set out to discover why his tormentors were intent on destroying his faith. When he read the early writings of Karl Marx he discovered that Marx wasn't an atheist; he was a Satanist. Karl Marx didn't believe in communism, but he embraced it in an effort to destroy Christian civilization.[77]

Mikhail Gorbachev was the dictator of the USSR and the director of the Soviet KGB before he came to the United States. Maurice Strong, Stephen Rockefeller, and Mikhail Gorbachev wrote the Earth Charter, which calls for a world government and a new spirituality. Gorbachev's State of the World Forum meetings always have an underlying theme of occultism.[78]

I mentioned a letter sent by the Lucis Trust that referred to the great Ashram of Sanat Kumara and to the Light. Sanat Kumara is an anagram for Satan; the Light represents Lucifer.[79]

Some people believe that government officials are covering up the fact that UFOs are real and that aliens have visited our planet. Nothing could be further from the truth. UFOs are probably demonic manifestations, and aliens are either demons or fallen angels.[80]

Barbara Marx Hubbard is one of the leaders of the New

Age movement.[81] In her book, *The Book of Co-Creation*, she discusses the hidden meaning of the Revelation of St. John the Divine. Her manuscript was channeled by a spirit she called The Christ Light. She quoted from Revelation 6:8:

> And I looked, and behold a pale horse: and his name that sat on him was Death, and Hell followed with him. And Power was given unto them over the fourth part of the earth, to kill with sword, and with hunger, and with death, and with the beasts of the earth.[82]

The Christ Light explained the true meaning of that passage:

> Out of the full spectrum of human personality, one-fourth is electing to transcend with all their heart, mind and spirit. . . . One-fourth is resistant to election. They are unattracted by life ever-evolving. Their higher self is unable to penetrate the density of their mammalian senses. They cannot be reached. . . . They are defective seeds. . . .
>
> Now, as we approach the quantum shift from creature-human to co-creative human . . . the destructive one-fourth must be eliminated from the social body. . . . Fortunately you, dearly beloveds, are not responsible for this act. We are. We are in charge of God's selection process for planet Earth. He selects, we destroy. We are the riders of the pale horse, Death.
>
> We come to bring death to those who are unable to know God. We do this for the sake of the world. . . .
>
> The riders of the pale horse are about to pass among you. Grim reapers, they will separate the wheat from the chaff. This is the most painful period in the history of humanity. . . .
>
> You do not have to participate in the destruction. You

are to be responsible for the construction which shall be-
gin as the tribulations come to an end.[83]

I believe the spirit that channeled those words was a demon.
Barbara Marx Hubbard has been a consultant for our Department of Defense, and she ran for the Democrat Party's
vice-presidential nomination in 1984. You can access her web
site on the Internet.

Martin Luther understood the battle we face when he
wrote:

A mighty fortress is our God,
A bulwark never failing;
Our helper He, amid the flood
Of mortal ills prevailing:
For still our ancient foe
Doth seek to work us woe;
His craft and power are great,
And, armed with cruel hate,
On earth is not his equal.

Did we in our own strength confide,
Our striving would be losing;
Were not the right Man on our side,
The Man of God's own choosing:
Dost ask who that may be?
Christ Jesus, it is He;
Lord Sabaoth, His name,
From age to age the same,
And He must win the battle.

And though this world, with devils filled,
Should threaten to undo us,

We will not fear, for God hath willed
His truth to triumph through us;
The Prince of Darkness grim—
We tremble not for him;
His rage we can endure,
For lo, his doom is sure,
One little word shall fell him.

That word above all earthly powers,
No thanks to them abideth;
The Spirit and the gifts are ours
Through Him who with us sideth:
Let goods and kindred go,
This mortal life also;
The body they may kill:
God's truth abideth still,
His kingdom is forever. Amen.[84]

Saint Paul warned us about the spiritual forces that are aligned against us when he wrote:

> Put on the whole armour of God, that ye may be able to stand against the wiles of the devil. For we wrestle not against flesh and blood, but against principalities, against powers, against the rulers of the darkness of this world, against spiritual wickedness in high places. Wherefore take unto you the whole armour of God, that ye may be able to withstand in the evil day, and having done all, to stand.[85]

God and Satan are involved in a cosmic struggle for the souls of mankind, and each of us is involved whether we want to be or not. The battle is being waged in our courts, our media, our schools, our banks, our military, our churches, and in our government. It appears that God has given Satan free reign to do as he pleases to determine how we will respond. Perhaps these are the last days, and nothing can be done to turn back the tide of destruction that Barbara Marx Hubbard and her followers anticipate, but who can be certain, since Jesus told His disciples that no man knows when He will return. What will happen if Christ returns thirty years after America has fallen, and billions of people have been slaughtered because we were too busy to be involved? If that happens, how will we justify our lack of concern? Some people who say nothing can be done are cowards; others are working for the enemy. What are we to do? In Ezekiel 3 and Ezekiel 33, we are told to be watchmen, and to warn others. If we remain silent, their blood will be on our hands. We are to be involved, just as the servant who was given one talent to invest for his Master should have been involved. Because he did nothing, he was punished. We are to pray as if everything is up to God, and work as if everything depends on us. Christians will face persecution in the days that lie ahead, and we must prepare ourselves and our families for that eventuality. We are engaged in a battle for the hearts and minds of men. We are to do our best, and recognize that ultimately the battle is the Lord's.

This story began with three poems. The first poem was written by Alfred Lord Tennyson, who was involved in the occult. His poem offered a vision of Utopia where all men will live happily under a world government.

The second poem was written by Rudyard Kipling. Almost all of Kipling's early books had swastikas engraved on their covers because he was both a Mason and an occultist.[86]

The third poem was written by James Russell Lowell to immortalize the eternal battle between God and Satan. Part of his poem was incorporated into one of the great hymns of

Christendom, and I conclude my story with his words.

> Once to every man and nation
> Comes the moment to decide,
> In the strife of truth with falsehood,
> For the good or evil side;
> Some great cause, God's new messiah,
> Offering each the bloom or blight,
> And the choice goes by forever
> 'Twixt that darkness and that light.
> Then to side with truth is noble,
> When we share her wretched crust,
> Ere her cause bring fame and profit,
> And 'tis prosperous to be just;
> Then it is the brave man chooses,
> While the coward stands aside,
> Till the multitude make virtue
> Of the faith they had denied.
>
> By the light of burning martyrs,
> Christ, thy bleeding feet we track,
> Toiling up new Calvaries ever
> With the Cross that turns not back.
> New occasions teach new duties:
> Time makes ancient good uncouth;
> They must upward still and onward
> Who would keep abreast of truth.
>
> Though the cause of evil prosper,
> Yet 'tis truth alone is strong;
> Though her portion be the scaffold
> And upon the throne be wrong,
> Yet that scaffold sways the future,

And, behind the dim unknown,
Standeth God within the shadow,
Keeping watch above his own.[87]

Footnotes

1. Carroll Quigley, *The Anglo-American Establishment*, Books in Focus, 1981, p. 3
2. Ibid., p. 32.
3. Ibid., p. 265.
4. Carroll Quigley, *Tragedy and Hope*, The Macmillan Company, New York, 1966, p. 1248.
5. *The Anglo-American Establishment*, op cit., Publisher's Note.
6. Ibid., preface, p. xi.
7. Ibid., preface, p. x.
8. Ibid., p. 5.
9. Ibid., p. 3.
10. Ibid., preface, p. ix.
11. Frederic Whyte, *The Life of William T. Stead*, Houghton Mifflin, London, pp. 208–209.
12. Rhodes *Confession of Faith*, available from Alfred Milner's papers at Rhodes House, Professor Quigley's papers at Georgetown University, or in the Sustainable Development Syllabus from Radio Liberty at P.O. Box 13, Santa Cruz, California 95063. See Also: *The Anglo-American Establishment*, op cit., p. 34.
13. Quigley, *Tragedy and Hope*, op cit., p. 950.
14. Quigley, *The Anglo-American Establishment*, op cit., chapter three.
15. H. G. Wells, *Experiment in Autobiography*, The Macmillan Company, New York, 1934, p. 651.
16. Quigley, *The Anglo-American Establishment*, op cit., pp. 30, 31, 58, 137.

17. Quigley, *Tragedy and Hope,* op cit., p. 684.

18. Letter to H. G. Wells from Winston Churchill, October 15, 1941, H. G. Wells' Papers. Available to researchers from Radio Liberty.

19. H. G. Wells, *The New Machiavelli,* John Lane The Bodley Head, Vigo Street, London, W. MCMXI, pp. 340–341. See Also: John Barnes and David Nicholson, *The Leo Amery Diaries,* Volume I:1896–1929, Hutchinson, London, 1980, p. 41.

20. Frederic Howe, *The Confessions of a Reformer,* Charles Scribner's Sons, New York, 1925, pp. 291–292.

21. Ibid., pp. 295–296.

22. Dan Smoot, *The Invisible Government,* Western Islands, Boston, 1965, p. 7.

23. Quigley, *Tragedy and Hope,* op cit., pp. 951–952.

24. Letter from William P. Dodd to Colonel House, October 29, 1936, Sterling Library at Yale University, New Haven, Connecticut: Jim Marrs, *Rule By Secrecy,* Harper Collins, 2000, pp. 181–189. See also: Charles Higham, *Trading with the Enemy,* Delacorte Press, 1983, preface.

25. Quigley, *Tragedy and Hope,* op cit., pp. 951–952.

26. Phyllis Schlafly and Chester Ward, *Kissinger on the Couch,* Arlington House, New Rochelle, New York, 1975, pp. 150–151.

27. Quigley, *The Anglo-American Establishment,* op cit., p. 3. See also: Frank Aydelotte, *The Vision of Cecil Rhodes,* Oxford University Press, London, 1946, p. 5.

28. Quigley, *Tragedy and Hope,* op cit., p. 130.

29. Dennis Cuddy, *Secret Records Revealed,* Hearthstone Publishing, Ltd., Oklahoma City, 1994, 1999, p. 9. See also: *Encyclopedia Americana,* International Edition, Volume 25, 1966, p. 422. See also: Frederic Whyte, *The Life of W. T. Stead,* Volume II, Houghton Mifflin, p. 26.

30. John Daniel, *Scarlet and the Beast*, Volume I, JKI Publishing, Tyler Texas, 1995, pp. 531–534.

31. Ibid.

32. Rhodes *Confession of Faith*, op cit.

33. Quigley, *The Anglo-American Establishment*, op cit., pp. 497, 494, 496, 525, 532, 536-537. See also: *The Life of William T. Stead*, op cit., pp. 26–27.

34. Quigley, *The Anglo-American Establishment*, op cit., pp. 31–32.

35. *Encyclopedia Americana*, op cit., volume 25, p. 422.

36. Tom C. McKenney, *Please Tell Me*, Huntington House, 1994, pp. 61–72.

37. Ibid., pp. 197–198.

38. Ibid., p. 198.

39. Ibid., p. 198.

40. McKenney, *Please Tell Me*, pp. 18, 28, 33, 77, 79, 205–208. See also: Rex Hutchens, *A Bridge to Light*, The Supreme Council of the Inspectors General Knights Commander of the House of the Temple of Solomon of the 33rd Degree. . . . 1988, pp. vii, ix.

41. Albert Pike, *Morals and Dogma*, Supreme Council of the Thirty Third Degree of the Scottish Rite, 1871, pp. 105, 819, 781, 219, 840.

42. Manly P. Hall, *Lectures on Ancient Philosophy*, Philosophical Research Society, Inc., Los Angeles, California, 1984, p. 409.

43. Corinne McLaughlin and Gordon Davidson, *Spiritual Politics*, Ballantine Books, 1994, p. 297.

44. John Robinson, *Born in Blood*, M. Evans and Company, New York, 1989, p. xiv.

45. McLaughlin & Davidson, *Spiritual Politics*, op cit., p. 297.

46. Manly P. Hall, *The Secret Destiny of America*, The Philosophical Research Society, Inc., Los Angeles, California

90027, 1944, p. 72.

47. Ibid., p. 126.

48. Ibid., p. 174.

49. McLaughlin & Davidson, *Spiritual Politics*, op cit., p. 249. See also: *Scarlet and the Beast*, op cit., p.174.

50. Robinson, *Born in Blood*, op cit., pp. xi–xix.

51. Ibid.

52. Michael Howard, *The Occult Conspiracy*, Destiny Books, Rochester, Vermont, 1989, pp. 30–41.

53. Hall, *Lectures on Ancient Philosophy*, op cit., p. 438.

54. Pike, *Morals and Dogma*, op cit., p. 840.

54. Ibid., p. 841.

55. Ibid., p. 839.

56. Pike, *Morals and Dogma*, op cit., p. 567.

57. Ibid., p. 321.

58. Manly P. Hall, *The Lost Keys of Freemasonry*, Macoy Publishing, Richmond, Virginia, 1923, p. 48.

59. Marion Meade, *Madame Blavatsky*, G. P. Putnam's Sons, New York, 1980, pp. 180–181. See also: A&E video production: *The Search for Lost Atlantis*. See also: George Grant, *Killer Angel*, Ars Vitae Press, 1995, p. 90.

60. H. P. Blavatsky, *The Secret Doctrine*, volume II, Theosophical University Press, 1888, p. 243.

61. Ibid., p. 513.

62. James Wardner, *Unholy Alliances*, Self-Published, 1996, identifies Roosevelt, Truman, Ford, and Johnson as Masons. President Reagan was inducted into the 33rd Degree while in office.

63. Paul Fisher, *Behind the Lodge Door*, Tan Books, Rockford, Illinois, 1994, p. 244.

64. C. William Smith, "God's Plan in America," *The New Age Magazine*, September 1950, volume LVIII, No. 9, p. 531. See also: Des Griffin, *Storming the Gates of Hell*, Emis-

sary Publications, Clackamas, Oregon 97015, pp. 82–83.

65. Daniel, *Scarlet and the Beast,* op cit., p. 334.

65. McLaughlin & Davidson, *Spiritual Politics,* op cit., p. 278. See also: Jim Marrs, *Rule by Secrecy,* op cit., pp. 181–182. See also: Higham, *Trading with the Enemy,* op cit., preface.

66. Quigley, *Tragedy and Hope,* op cit., p. 952. See also: McLaughlin & Davidson, *Spiritual Politics,* op cit., p. 278.

67. James Pool and Suzanne Pool, *Who Financed Hitler,* The Dial Press, New York, 1978, pp. 85–130.

68. McLaughlin & Davidson, *Spiritual Politics,* op cit., pp. 219, 169. See also: Daniel, *Scarlet and the Beast,* op cit., pp. 582–583. See also: Rene Wormser, *Foundations: Their Power and Influence,* Devin-Adair Co., New York, pp. 45–47, 332–336.

69. McLaughlin & Davidson, *Spiritual Politics,* op cit., p. 209; Daniel, *Scarlet and the Beast,* op cit., p. 429.; Wormser, *Foundations: Their Power and Influence,* op cit., pp. 204–205; John McManus, *Changing Commands,* The John Birch Society, Appleton, Wisconsin, 1995, p. 87.

70. McLaughlin & Davidson, *Spiritual Politics,* op cit., p. 248. The author found a copy of *The Protocols* among Colonel House's papers at the Sterling Library at Yale University.

71. Daniel, *Scarlet and the Beast,* op cit., pp. 550, 625, 627, 885.

72. *Encyclopedia Americana,* op cit., volume 6, p. 663a, and volume 29, p. 297.

73. Gen. Albert C. Wedemeyer, *Wedemeyer Reports!,* The Devin-Adair Company, New York, 1958, pp. 231, 242. See also: Personal communication with General Albert Wedemeyer, 1980.

74. Michael J. Neufeld and Michael Berenbaum, *The Bombing of Auschwitz,* St. Martin's Press: discusses the fact

that the Allies refused to bomb Auschwitz and stop the Holocaust.

75. Miranda J. Green, *The World of the Druids*, Thames and Hudson, 1997, p. 170. See also: Daniel, *Scarlet and the Beast*, pp. 353, 472, 511, 598–599.

76. Hall, *The Lost Keys of Freemasonry*, op cit., p. 48.

77. Richard Wurmbrand, *Marx and Satan*, Living Sacrifice Book Company, Bartlesville, Oklahoma, 1986, pp. 20–35.

78. Radio Liberty interview with Joan Peros, available from Radio Liberty.

79. Letter from Lucis Trust, 120 Wall Street, 24th Floor, New York, New York 10005, announcing Festivals and Conferences, 1999.

80. Paul Christopher, *Alien Intervention*, Huntington House, 1998, p. 80.

81. The Foundation for Conscious Evolution, P.O. Box 4698, Santa Barbara, California 93140, provides up-to-date information on Barbara Marx Hubbard.

82. Barbara Marx Hubbard, *The Book of Co-Creation*, self-published, p. 59.

83. Ibid., pp. 60–61.

84. Charles Johnson, "A Mighty Fortress Is Our God," *One Hundred and One Famous Hymns*, p. 21.

85. King James Bible, Ephesians 6:11–13.

86. Cuddy, *Secret Records Revealed*, op cit., p. 33.

87. Johnson, *One Hundred and One Famous Hymns*, op cit., p. 87.

index

German High Command 60, 61
German knight 77
German medal 62
German secret society 78
German soldiers 30
Germany 41, 81, 92, 101, 106, 112
Gilman family 79. *See also* Skull and
Bones
Global Biodiversity Assessment Report 43.
See also Strong, Maurice
global feudalism 34
global governance 41, 42
global government 38, 73
global warming 27
Gnostic(s) 77, 126
God 49, 73, 130, 134, 136, 137
God and prayer from public schools 24,
50, 73. *See also* prayer out of our schools
God and Satan 23, 137
God of Darkness 127. *See also* light and
darkness
God of Light 127. *See also* light
God, prayer, and the Bible 129
God's Plan in America 142. *See also* Smith,
William C.
Goethe 57
gold 117
gold mines 94
Goldman-Sachs 35, 36
Goldsborough, Robert 84
Goldwater, Barry 26, 37, 38, 40, 82, 83, 84
Goncz, Arpad 42
good and evil 23
Gorbachev, Mikhail 41, 44, 45, 133
Gotha 58
Goulevitch, A 67, 87. *See also* Milner, Lord
Alfred
government of the world. *See* Truman,
Harry
Grant, George 89, 142
Great Architect of the Universe 74, 121.
See also Masons
Great Britain 12, 18, 34, 63, 96, 110, 111,
112, 114, 118
Great Light, The 130
Great Seal 76, 81, 123, 124
Great Trust, The 15. *See also* Bellamy,
Edward
Greek 36
Green, Miranda J. 144
Greening, The 84. *See also* Abraham, Larry
Greenspan, Alan 35
Grenfell 96
Grey, Albert 109. *See also* Junta of three
Grey, Edward 103, 110
Griffin, Des 142
Griffin, G. Edward 68, 83, 87, 88. *See also*
The Creature from Jekyll Island

Grim reapers 134
Group, the 107, 108. *See also* Rhodes,
Cecil John
Guaranty Trust Company 70, 100. *See also*
May, Max
guns without bolts 20

H
Hall, Manly P. 8, 24, 74, 76, 77, 88, 122,
124, 125, 126, 128, 132, 141, 142, 144
Hammer, Armand 71
Hanoch and Trismegistus 127. *See also*
Science of Abraham and Orpheus, of
Confucius and ZOROASTER
harbinger of light 128. *See also* light; light
and darkness
Harriman, Averill 71
Harriman family 79. *See also* Skull and
Bones
Harvard 29
Harvard Socialism 67
Havel, Vaclav 42
Hays, Wayne 53
185-minute testimony 53.
hell 134
Herder 57
Hermetic Freemasons 58, 78, 122, 126,
129
hidden force 79. *See also* dark forces; dark
spiritual forces; force
hierarchy 54, 55
Hierarchy and Humanity 54. *See also*
Lucis Trust
Higham, Charles 140, 143
Hinduism 80
Hitler, Adolph 21, 62, 81, 99, 100, 101,
106, 128, 131
Hitler's death camps 81
Holocaust 81, 132, 144
Holy Inquisition 125
Holy Land 124
Holy Scriptures 77
Holy Word 77
homosexuality 49
Hoover, Herbert 69, 70, 87, 104
Hoover, J. Edgar 85
Hoover Institute 61. *See also* Sutton,
Antony C.
Hotel Chatham 113
House, Colonel Edward Mandell 30, 63,
64, 65, 66, 69, 83, 87, 97, 100, 112, 114,
131, 140, 143
House of Rothschild 35
House of the Temple in Washington,
D.C. 120
HUAC (House Un-American Activities
Committee) 99
Howard, Michael 142